环球雅思学校雅思（IELTS）考试指定辅导用书

MW01712100

雅思写作机经词汇

最新版 融入剑9

李 静◎编著

WRITING

IELTS

机经与词汇的完美结合 首印狂销上万册

◇ 分类撷取高频词汇，雅思写作，轻松搞定
◇ 海量精选经典例句，高分佳句，精彩复制
◇ 匠心独运写作提示，写作玄机，一语道破
◇ 链接机经关键词汇，素材思路，全面突破

浙江工商大学出版社
ZHEJIANG GONGSHANG UNIVERSITY PRESS

图书在版编目(CIP)数据

雅思写作机经词汇 / 李静编著. -- 杭州 : 浙江工商大学出版社, 2013.4（2013.12重印）

ISBN 978-7-81140-712-9

Ⅰ. ①雅… Ⅱ. ①李… Ⅲ. ①IELTS - 词汇 - 自学参考资料 Ⅳ. ①H313

中国版本图书馆CIP数据核字(2013)第036171号

雅思写作机经词汇

李　静　编著

特约策划　北京环球卓尔英才文化传播有限公司
策划编辑　李晟月　吕颜辉
责任编辑　周敏燕
封面设计　王　辉
责任印制　汪　俊
出版发行　浙江工商大学出版社
（杭州市教工路198号 邮政编码 310012）
（E-mail: zjgsupress@163.com）
（网址：http://www.zjgsupress.com）
电话：0571-88904980, 88831806（传真）
印　　刷　北京合众伟业印刷有限公司
开　　本　880mm × 1230mm 1/32
印　　张　9
字　　数　219 千字
版 印 次　2013 年 5 月第 1 版　2013 年 12 月第 2 次印刷
书　　号　ISBN 978-7-81140-712-9
定　　价　19.80元

浙江工商大学出版社营销部邮购电话　0571-88804227

环球雅思图书编委会核心小组

推荐序

环球雅思学校自2001年成立以来，带领一批又一批资深、优秀的教师帮助众多雅思考生走进自己心中的教育圣堂。怀着对雅思教学一贯的热情，环雅的优秀教师们不断跟踪雅思考试的变化，潜心教研，著书立说，为更多学生送去考雅真经。“雅思机经词汇”即是融多位优秀教师多年教学精华的作品。这套丛书的作者均有多年的雅思教学经验，他们非常清楚学生学习中的难点，其中词汇的积累和正确使用正是所有学生不断提升雅思分数的关键，掌握了大量雅思特有词汇可以帮助学生搭建起通向高分的阶梯。源于此，这些优秀的教师们在课外投入了大量时间整理近十年来的雅思真题机经词汇，携手向全国考生推出“雅思机经词汇”系列。

“雅思机经词汇”系列第一版是在2010年出版的，由于该系列内囊括的词汇均为考试中的高频词汇，且分类合理，注释清晰，和正式考试的契合度高，大大提升了学生词汇学习的效率，所以，“雅思机经词汇”系列一经问世，就受到了不同水平段学生的关注和好评。环雅的优秀教师再接再厉，很快整理和推出2013版的“雅思机经词汇”（最新版）。最新版沿袭了第一版的一些特点，同时具备以下几个优势：

① 更新了2010–2013年的词汇及机经回顾，并增加了“剑8”“剑9”中的词汇、例句、高分答案、范

文材料等；所有词汇均为近7年雅思机经中出现频率最高的词汇

② 体例科学、合理：除了精心筛选的核心单词之外，配有“机经回顾”、留学背景知识补充、“实时检测”等备考和帮助词汇记忆的部分

③ 小巧便携，便于考生利用鸡肋时间扩大词汇量，备考雅思

本书的出版相信给忙碌准备考试的考生们插上一双梦想的翅膀，助力他们在准备考试的时间内和正式考试中能披荆斩棘，最终展翅高飞。祝贺各位教师作者在学术上再攀高峰，也代表环球雅思感谢他们给环球以至于全国的学生送来的这套好书！

环球天下教育集团副总裁

张晓飞

2013年4月于北京

前言

今闻出版《雅思写作机经词汇》第二版，非常欣喜。感谢本书出版以来众多读者的厚爱。

第二版《雅思写作机经词汇》在保留了第一版所有的精华基础上，更新机经话题并更新部分词汇，给读者以最优秀的材料。

本书共分为三个单元，第一个单元是雅思写作的小作文部分，按照A类图表作文和G类书信作文的顺序展开。A类图表作文词汇是要掌握文章开篇点题关键词、主体段关键词、变化趋势关键词、变化程度关键词、极值描述关键词等。G类书信作文词汇是要掌握感谢信、投诉信、道歉信、询问信、申请信、推荐信、邀请信和求职信等雅思写作常考书信的高频词汇。第二单元根据雅思大作文的题目分类，以主题词汇的形式，即先确定类别，再分层侧重、多次接触，帮助大家熟练掌握雅思写作常考题目及高频词汇。第三单元主攻文章的逻辑性，这部分内容能够帮助大家理清英文写作逻辑，正确使用作文的路标词，以增强作文的逻辑关联。

《雅思写作机经词汇》的**特色之一：经典例句**，各主词条下的例句均取自雅思写作经典范文。研习雅思写作经典范文和例句，是增强考生遣词造句能力的一种最有效的方法。**特色之二：链接机经关键词**，帮助考生突破雅思写作词汇，辅助考生梳理写作思路的同时，了解写作常用词汇和必背词汇。**特色之三：写作提示**，将作文题目及单词结合成一体，延伸思路，拓展写作思维。

对于雅思写作词汇，希望大家能够坚持大量重复的记忆，毕竟，只有我们的作文词汇资源丰富、言之有物，才能得到理想的分数。

本书的出版，首先要感谢环球教育集团总裁张永琪先生、董事长张晓东女士、北京环球雅思学校校长司晗女士以及环球卓尔公司刘海华总经理对我的支持与帮助。同时，还要感谢环球卓尔公司的编辑同仁，本书从调研论证、编写完成到出版，前后历时一年多，经过无数次的讨论、否定、修改与校验，她们为本书的出版付出了辛勤的劳动。

在本书的编辑过程中，纪晓琳、张永财、岳纲举、李月、刘建芳、张平、吕文萍、王玉梅、宋鑫和赵于飞也参与了资料收集及部分编写工作，在此一并致谢。

由于笔者水平有限，难免出现纰漏与不足，恳请批评指正。

李 静

2013年4月

目录

Unit 1　Writing Task 1 高分词汇

Unit 2　Writing Task 2 高频词汇

Unit 3 逻辑词汇联盟

Unit 1

Writing Task 1 高分词汇

本单元主要介绍了在A类图表作文和G类书信作文中常用的高分词汇。A类图表作文，要求文字简练，客观地反映图表的基本内容，并根据图表所表示的变化趋势或特点得出合理结论。图表作文的词汇主要从开篇点题关键词、主体段关键词、变化趋势关键词、变化程度关键词、极值描述关键词和对比描述关键词等方面介绍A类图表作文的高分词汇。G类书信作文的词汇主要介绍感谢信、投诉信、道歉信、询问信、求职信、申请信、推荐信、邀请信和建议信等作文中常用的高分词汇。各种书信之间有着密切关系：如感谢信是基础，因为很多信件的结尾处都要表示期盼回复或者感谢；投诉信和道歉信正好是两个相反的过程；求职信、申请信、询问信和邀请信等都是想从收信人处获得信息。

1. A类图表词汇

考点回顾

Table （表格）	20100619 欧洲咖啡和香蕉的销售情况 20100415 北美国家家庭构成的变化
Bar Chart （柱状图）	20100508 欧洲不同年龄段的人的每周工作时间 20100130 学生上学的交通方式
Pie Chart （饼图）	20121011 澳洲年轻人毕业后工作、继续学习、失业对比
Line/Curve Graph （线形图/曲线图）	20130406 美国、加拿大和澳大利亚的移民数变化
Flow Chart （流程图）	20130223 雨水变成饮用水的过程

开篇点题关键词

illustrate ['iləstreit] *vt.* 阐明，举例说明，图解

拓 illustrated *adj.* 有插图的

illustration *n.* 图表；例证；阐明

同 show *vt.&vi.* 显示；说明

demonstrate *vt.* 证明；说明

例 The graph illustrates changes in the amount of beef, lamb, chicken, and fish consumed in a particular European country between 1979 and 2004.

该图表描述了在1979年至2004年间，欧洲某国在牛肉、羊肉、鸡肉和鱼肉上消耗量的变化。

写作提示

雅思写作题目中常用show或者give information about 表示描述之意，开篇点题常用转述题目的方法来介绍图表类型及描述内容，其间会常用到具有“描述”含义的表达。

breakdown ['breikdaun] *n.* 分析，概要

例 Please give me a breakdown of those income tax totals. 请给我一份所得税的细目表。

concerning [kən'sə:niŋ] *prep.* 关于，就……而言

同 respecting *prep.* 关于，就……而言

regarding *prep.* 关于，至于

用 give/offer/provide information concerning

有关……的信息

例 The bar chart gives information concerning the change of marriage and divorce between 1970 and 2000 in USA. 该柱状图描述了在1970年到2000年间，美国结婚和离婚人数上的变化。

写作提示

concerning 一词使图表作文更加具体化，使读者一目了然。concerning后面所写的内容是图表主要描述的对象。

consumption [kən'sʌmpʃən] *n.*（能量、食物或材料的）消耗量，消耗

拓 consume *vt.* 消耗，消费

用 the consumption of water = water consumption 水的消耗量

consumption level 消费水平

consumption pattern 消费模式

consumption structure 消费结构

例 Fuel consumption has risen dramatically in the last few years. 过去几年燃料消耗量急剧增加。

写作提示

consumption与consume的词性转换

一般而言，动词的过去分词具备形容词性质，能与名词一样修饰其他名词，从某种意义上来说sth. consumption = sth. consumed。例：water consumption=water consumed，the consumption of fish = fish consumed。又如：剑1Test 1的Task 1的写作原题为…The graph shows the trends in consumption of fast foods. 考官范文第一句则改为The chart shows that high income earners consumed considerably more fast foods…可见除了同义词替换，也可采取词性转换的策略。

expenditure [iks'penditʃə] *n.*（时间、金钱、劳力等的）消耗，花费

拓 expend *vt.* 花费，消耗；expendable *adj.* 可消费的

同 spending *n.* 花费，开销

expense *n.* 消费，开支

consumption *n.* 消耗量，消耗

用 the expenditure of time/money 花费时间/金钱

例 Food always accounted for comparatively a majority in the average family expenditure in Britain. 食物在普通的英国家庭消费中占据了相对很大的比例。

demand [di'mɑ:nd] *n.* 需求，需要

同 need *n.* 需要，要求

requirement *n.* 要求，需要

用 the demand for sth. 对……的需求

supply and demand 供给与需求

例 The demand for electricity in winter varies between 45,000 units and 30,000 units.冬天用电量的需求在45000和30000个单位之间变化。

data ['deitə] *n.* 数据，数字

同 figure *n.* 数字；number *n.* 数字

例 The data shows the differences between developing countries and industrialised countries' participation in education and science. 该数据表明发展中国家和工业化发达国家的科教发展存在差异。

amount [ə'maunt] *n.* 数量，总额，总数

例 The graph shows how the amount of water used worldwide changed between 1900 and 2000. 该图表描述了1900年到2000年间世界用水量的变化。

category ['kætigəri] *n.* 类别，种类

拓 categorise *vt.* 把……归类

同 type *n.* 类型，品种；group *n.*（人或物）群，组，类

用 in category 在……类别中

the category of ……的类别

例 In the unemployed and retired categories, leisure time showed an increase for both sexes, as might have been expected.
在失业及退休群体中，正像所预计的那样，男性及女性拥有的闲暇时间有所增加。

item ['aitəm] *n.* 项；条款；项目

用 durable consumer items (goods) 耐用消费品

例 The picture shows how worldwide water consumption in three items changed during 10 years.
图中描述了10年间，全世界范围内在三个方面水资源的消耗量。

feature ['fi:tʃə] *n.* 特征，特色

同 trait *n.* 特征，特点
characteristic *n.* 特征，特性

用 the main feature 主要特征

例 The table illustrates the main features of the underground railway systems in 6 cities.
该图描述了6个城市地铁系统的主要特点。

percentage [pə'sentidʒ] *n.* 比例

同 proportion *n.* 比例；ratio *n.* 比率，比例

用 the percentage remained steady at… 比例稳定在……
the percentage of…is slightly larger than that of… ……的比例稍微高出……

例 The numbers are small in percentage terms, but significant.
按百分比来说，这些数目并不大，但意义重大。

pattern ['pætən] *n.* 型，样式，方式，形式

同 model *n.* 典型，样式

用 the similar pattern was found in… 情形相近

例 We can see a similar pattern in the second graph, which shows that the number of people working as

scientists and technicians in industrialised countries increased from 55 to 1, 000 people between 1980 and 1990, while the number in developing countries went from 12 to 20.
从第二个图表中可以看出相似的情况，工业化国家的科技人员的数量在1980年至1990年间从55人上升至1000人，而发展中国家的数量从12人上升至20人。

status ['steitəs] *n.* 身份，地位，职位；情形，状况

同 position *n.* 地位；职位；rank *n.* 地位；等级
grade *n.* 等级，级别

例 The two bar charts illustrate the secondary and higher education status respectively in four different countries.
两个柱状图将四个国家的中等教育和高等教育的状况分别进行了描述。

namely ['neimli] *adv.* 即，也就是

例 The table compares four indicators among five countries in terms of living standard in 1982, namely, Bangladesh, Bolivia, Egypt, Indonesia and USA.
该表格就1982年五个国家生活水平的四个指标进行了比较，这五个国家分别是孟加拉国、玻利维亚、埃及、印度尼西亚及美国。

from...onwards 从……开始

例 From 1950 onwards, industrial water use grew steadily to just over 1,000 km^3. 从1950年开始，工业用水稳步增长到1000立方米以上。

span [spæn] *n.* 持续时间，时间阶段；*vt.*（时间）持续

拓 over the period from...to...
从……到……的一段时间

during the period from… to…
从……到……的时间段
during the period between …and…
在……和……的时间段
during the period starting from…
从……的一段时间

用 over a span of …years 在……年的时间内

例 His research in cancer that spanned 15 years has made considerable headway in the end. 他对癌症持续15年的研究终于取得了极大的进展。

typical ['tipikəl] *adj.* 典型的，有代表性的；特有的，独特的

拓 typically *adv.* 典型地，有代表性地
typify *vt.* 代表

同 characteristic *adj.* 典型的
distinctive *adj.* 有特色的
representative *adj.* 典型的，有代表性的

用 a typical example 一个典型的例子

例 The chart shows the number of hours enjoyed by men and women in a typical week in 1998 to 1999, according to gender and employment status.
根据性别及就业状况，图表显示了从1998年至1999年男性与女性一周内空余时间的情况。

in terms of 在……方面，就……来说；关于……，根据

同 in respect of 在……方面

例 The chart gives information about post-school qualifications in terms of the different levels of further education reached by men and women in Australia in 1999. 该图表描述了1999年澳大利亚男女不同学历层次的情况。

range [reindʒ] *n.* 变化幅度；范围；*vi.*（在……范围内）变动，变化

同 scope *n.* 范围；extent *n.* 程度

用 a range of 很多，一系列

range from...to... 变化范围从……到……

in range with 和……并列

within range of 在……范围以内

range...between 范围在……之间不等

例 The chart shows that Britain, among the four European countries listed, has spent most heavily on the range of consumer goods included.

该图表表明在列举的四个欧洲国家中，英国在各种消耗上的花费比重最大。

durable ['djuərəbl] *adj.* 耐用的，持久的；*n.* 耐用品

用 durable goods 耐用品

durable consumer goods = consumer durables

耐用消费品

例 The chart shows that the percentage of British household with a range of consumer durables steadily increased between 1972 and 1983.

该图描述了1972年至1983年间，英国家庭在耐用品上的消费比例稳步上升。

on a daily basis 每天

同 every day 每天

例 The trend line gives the information about how the electricity demands on a daily basis change in winter and summer.

该趋势图描述了冬天和夏天日消耗的电量的变化情况。

主体段关键词

according to 根据，按照，据……所说

同 as shown in… 如……所示

as can be seen from… 从……可以看出

用 according to gender and employment status

根据性别及就业状况

例 According to the table, the majority of people in England chose to travel for the purpose of visiting friends. 表格描述了大部分英国人旅行的目的是拜访朋友。

写作提示

according to这个短语可以放在主体段第一句开头，起着概括引领下文的作用。

It is clear from…that… 从……中可以清楚地看出……

同 It is manifest from…that…

从……中可以很明显地看出……

It is apparent from…that…

从……中可以清楚地看出……

It is noticeable that… 值得注意的一点是……

例 Overall, it is clear from statistics that by 2000 these two countries relied on different principal fuel sources: Australia relied on coal and France on nuclear power. 总之，从数据中很明显地看到截止到2000年时，两个国家依赖不同的能源。澳大利亚依赖于煤而法国依赖于核能。

to be more precise 具体来说，更确切地说

同 more precisely 更确切地说

to be more specific 更准确地说

to be more exact 更准确地说

more exactly 更准确地说

例 To be more precise, table tennis occupies the biggest part among the five types of sports, which is 32%. Then, football, which accounts for 25%, being in the second place.

具体来说，在五种运动中，乒乓球所占比例最大，为32%。其次是足球，所占比例为25%。

写作提示

图表中描写具体信息值时，to be more precise可以用来引出数据。举例时，大作文中常用for example之类的，而小作文描写重点数值时常用specifically等。如Specifically, France spends more on CDs and photographic film but less on tennis racquets than Italy does.

note ['nəut] *vt.* 注意，留意

拓 noted *adj.* 著名的，知名的

例 According to the line graph, a sharp rise in the number of private cars can be clearly noted. 根据此线形图，可以明显地看出私家车的数量急剧增加。

noticeable ['nəutisəbl] *adj.* 显而易见的，显著的，值得注意的

同 noteworthy *adj.* 值得注意的

例 It is noticeable that for both types of households with children, a higher than average proportion were living in poverty at this time.

值得注意的一点是在有子女的两类家庭模式中，其贫困比例要高于平均指数。

写作提示

突出强调某个极值或者变化趋势时，可以考虑使用下列句型：

It is noticeable that… 值得注意的是……
It should be noted that… 值得注意的是……
It is worth mentioning that… 值得一提的是……
It must be pointed out that… 应该指出的是……
It must be stressed out that… 应该指出的是……
What is noteworthy is that… 值得注意的是……

respectively [rɪ'spektɪvlɪ] *adv.* 分别地，各自地，独自地

拓 respective *adj.* 分别的，各自的

同 individually *adv.* 个别地，单独地

用 fall dramatically to…and…respectively
分别下降到
rise sharply to…and…respectively
分别上升到

例 However, those consisting of only one parent or a single adult had almost double this proportion of poor people, with 21% and 19% respectively.
然而，单亲家庭和单身成年人的贫困比例是这一数字的两倍，分别达到了21%和19%。

写作提示

当两个或两个以上的数值变化时，可用respectively描述，表示“分别地”，类似于namely的作用（参见P7）。

basically ['beisikəli] *adv.* 基本上，根本上

用 basically stable 基本稳定
basically unchanged 基本不变

例 The line graph is basically stable during the period.
该线形图在这一期间基本保持稳定。

generally ['dʒenərəli] *adv.* 通常，普遍地，一般地

同 in general 总之，通常

用 generally speaking 总体来说

例 Older people were generally less likely to be poor, though once again the trend favoured elderly couples (only 4%) rather than single elderly people (6%). 老年人不太容易成为贫困人口，该趋势再次表明老年夫妇的贫困比例是4%，而无伴侣的老年人的贫困比例为6%。

overall ['əuvərɔːl] *adj.* 全部的，全体的，一切在内的；*adv.* 总的说来

同 in conclusion 总之

It can be concluded that… 总的来说

to conclude 总而言之

用 with an overall upward trend 总体上呈上升趋势

例 Overall, the diagrams show that the cocoon stage of the silkworm can be used to produce silk cloth through a very simple process. 总之，流程图展现了在蚕茧阶段，蚕吐丝织布的过程很简单。

写作提示

overall是总结用词，经常用于结尾段。它也是形容词，例如overall trend（总结的趋势）。

average ['ævəridʒ] *n.* 平均，平均数；*adj.* 平均的，普通的

用 on average 平均；an average of 平均数

例 On average, 11% of all the households, comprising almost two million people, were in this position. 平均11%的家庭中，即包括大约200万人都处于这一水平。

total ['təutəl] *adj.* 全部的；*n.* 总数；*vt.* 共计，总计

拓 totally *adv.* 总数地，完全地

用 the total amount 总量

the total number 总数

in total 总共

grand total 共计，总数

total up 总数达

例 The foreign tourists totalled 500.

外国游客人数达500。

tend [tend] *vi.* 往往会，易于，倾向

拓 tendency *n.* 倾向，趋势

同 be likely to 倾向于，很有可能

用 tend to 多半，往往

例 Couples generally tended to be better off, with lower poverty levels for couples without children (7%) than those with children (12%).

结婚家庭往往都很富足，其中结婚而没有子女的家庭的贫困比例是7%，比有子女的家庭（12%）要低一些。

prone [prəun] *adj.* 倾向的，易于的，很可能的

同 be likely to 倾向于，很有可能

tend to 多半，往往

用 be prone to err 易犯过失

例 In China, Computer Industry and Finance were prone to be booming industries. 中国的计算机产业和金融业可能会蒸蒸日上。

predict [pri'dikt] *vt.&vi.* 预言，预测

同 foretell *vt.&vi.* 预言，预测

用 be predicted to do 据估计

例 A more dramatic rise is predicted between 2030 and 2040 in Japan, by which time it is thought that the proportion of elderly people will be similar in the three countries. 据估计，在2030年至2040年间，日本老年人口数会更快地上涨，到那时三个国家老年人口的比例会很相似。

be expected to do 有望，期望

同 be predicted to do 据预测；be supposed to do 应该

例 It indicates that the percentage of elderly people in all three countries is expected to increase to almost 25% of the respective population by the year 2040.

图表显示出在2040年三个国家的老年人口比例将会分别达到其总人口的25%。

spend [spend] *vt.&vi.* 花费，消耗，用尽（精力等）

拓 spending *n.* 花费，开销

例 The bar chart shows the amount of money spent on the fast foods according to three different income groups.

该柱状图描述了三种不同收入的家庭在快餐上的花费情况。

estimate ['estimeit] *vi.* 估计，估价；*vt.* 估计，判断，评价

用 estimate the cost of... 估计……的成本

例 The population of elderly is estimated to continue to increase until reaching a peak of 38.63 million in 2042 when it will start to decrease.

老年人口总数预计会持续上升，直到2042年达到峰值3863万，才会开始回落。

account for 共计达，（在数量、比例上）占……

同 occupy *vt.* 占据；take up 占据

例 Specifically, heating rooms and water account for the largest proportion of the electricity used while the need of ovens and washing machines makes up 17.5% of the total.

具体来说，房屋取暖及热水占了用电总量的最大部分，而炉具和洗衣机占了总数的17.5%。

comprise [kəm'praiz] *vt.* 包含，由……组成

用 be comprised of 由……组成

例 This month's figures are comprised in the total.
这个月的数字已包含在总数之内。

remainder [ri'meində] *n.* 余数，剩余物，其余的人

同 the remaining part 余下的部分

例 In 1980 Australia used coal as the main electricity source (50 units) and the remainder was produced from natural gas, hydro power (each producing 20 units) and oil (which produced only 10 units).
1980年，澳大利亚以煤炭为主要的电能来源（50单位），其余主要依赖于天然气、水力发电（均占20单位）和石油（仅占1单位）。

enjoy [in'dʒɔi] *vt.* 利用，享受，享有

同 share *vt.&vi.* 共享，分担

用 enjoy the most popularity 最受欢迎

例 Lastly, housewives enjoyed approximately fifty-four hours of leisure, on average.
最后，家庭主妇平均拥有近54小时的空余时间。

turn out 结果是，原来是

用 turn out to be the first 结果是第一
turn out to be the lowest 结果是最低的

例 The amount of water use in the city turned out to be the highest at the end of century.
在世纪末，城市用水量是最高的。

analysis [ə'næləsis] *n.* 分析，分解（复数analyses）

拓 analyse *vt.* 分析

例 The figures for the United States indicate the greatest number of prisoners compared to the other four countries but population size needs to be taken into account in this analysis. 和其他四个国家相比，美国的罪犯数量最多，但同时也应该将总人口考虑在内。

given ['givən] *adj.* 给定的

例 It is clear from the data given that there are some significant differences in spending habits within Europe. 根据给出的数据可以看出欧洲各个国家在消费习惯上有很大的不同。

in details 详细地

例 In details, the percentage at the age of 65 or more in Japan is predicted to rise to 27%. 具体来说，日本65岁以上的老年人预计会上升至27%。

popularity [ˌpɔpju'læriti] *n.* 普遍，流行，受欢迎

拓 popular *adj.* 流行的；popularise *vt.* 普及
popularisation *n.* 大众化，普及

用 enjoy the popularity 受欢迎
the popularity of... ……的流行

例 The consumption of hamburgers and pizza enjoyed the popularity in1985.
1985年汉堡和比萨的消耗量最多。

appear to 似乎，好像

同 be likely to do 很可能

例 Low income earners appear to spend less than other income groups on fast foods. 低收入家庭好像比其他类型的家庭在快餐上的花费要少些。

approximately [ə'prɔksimitli] *adv.* 大约

同 about *adv.* 大约
around *adv.* 大约
nearly *adv.* 几乎

例 By 2000, coal had become the fuel for more than 75% of electricity produced and only hydro continued to be another significant source supplying approximately 20%. 到2000年，超过75%的电力来源来自煤炭，水力发电仍保持第二大重要的电力来源，大约占20%。

写作提示

列举数据时都要加上“大约”一类的词，表示出一定的精准性。当然，有比“大约”更准确的词汇，如：刚刚超出：just over，just above；差一点不到：just under，just below。

变化趋势关键词

vary ['veəri] *vi.* 变化，有不同，相异

拓 various *adj.* 各种各样的
variety *n.* 多样，种类
variation *n.* 变化
variable *adj.* 易变的，多变的
variably *adv.* 易变地

同 change *vt.&vi.* 改变；alter *vt.&vi.* 改变
differ *vi.* 相异，不同

例 Based on the above figures, it can be concluded that the volume of TV sales varies with different seasons. 我们可以根据以上数据得出结论：电视机销售量随季节的变化而变化。

trend [trend] *n.* 趋势，倾向，走向

同 movement *n.* 动向，趋势
tendency *n.* 倾向，趋势
direction *n.* 方向

用 the general trend 总体趋势

the trend line 趋势图

例 The consumption of chicken, on the other hand, showed an upward trend.

相反地，鸡肉的消耗量呈上升的趋势。

写作提示

线型图重点是趋势(trend)的描写，经常和downward，upward搭配使用，如be on a downward trend, be on an upward trend等。

upward ['ʌpwəd] *adj.* 向上的，上升的；*adv.* 向上地

同 be on the rise 上升

用 be on an upward movement/trend

呈上升趋势

there is an upward trend in the number of...

……数量呈上升趋势

show an upward trend

呈上升趋势

例 The hours for the full-time of male workers was on an upward movement compared with the female counterparts. 与女性员工相比，男性全职员工的工作时间呈上升趋势。

downward ['daunwəd] *adj.* 向下的，下降的；*adv.* 向下地

同 be on the decline 下降趋势

用 be on a downward trend/movement 下降趋势

show a downward trend/movement 呈下降趋势

display a downward trend 呈下降趋势

例 The number of visitors from England to other countries showed a downward trend in 1999.

1999年英国的游客出现下降趋势。

increase [in'kri:s] *vi.&vt.* 增加，增大，增多

同 rise *vi.* 上升；go up 增长，上升；ascend *vt.&vi.* 上升

用 increase by... 增长了……

increase to... 增长到……

例 The data indicates that radio listeners increased substantially before 8:00 a.m., when the percentage reached to a peak of 27%.

数据表明收音机听众人数在早上8点前显著增加，比例达到了高峰时的27%。

写作提示

增加的数值用by，增加达到的数值用to，即增加的幅度用by，表示“增加了多少”；同理，减少的数值用by，减少达到的数值用to；从……增加或减少到……用from…to…。

rise [raiz] *vi.* 增加，提高

用 rise from…to… 从……上升到……

rise by… 增加了……

rise to… 增加到……

例 Between these years electricity production almost doubled, rising from 100 units to 170 units in Australia, and from 90 to 180 units in France.

在这些年间，电力供应量几乎翻番，澳大利亚从100单位上升到170单位，而法国从90单位上升到180单位。

shoot up 迅速上升

同 jump *vi.* 猛增；surge *vi.* 急剧上升；soar *vi.* 猛增

例 The number shoots up over the next two hours, peaking at 1000 at 8:00 a.m..

数量在接下来的两个小时急剧上升，在8点的时候达到最大值1000。

soar [sɔː] *vi.* 猛增；*n.*猛增，高涨

同 shoot up 迅速上升

skyrocket *vi.* 飞涨，突然高升

用 soar to almost… 猛增到将近……

例 By 2004 it had soared to almost 250 grams per person per week. 到2004年，鸡肉的消耗量飞涨到将近每人每周250克。

jump [dʒʌmp] *n.* 暴涨；*vi.* 暴涨，猛增

用 jump to… 猛增到……

例 The number jumped to its peak in a short period. 数量在很短的时间内达到顶峰。

decline [di'klain] *vi.* 下降；*n.* 下降，衰退

同 fall *vi.* 下降；*n.* 下降

drop *vi.* 下降；*n.* 下降

decrease *vt.&vi.* 减少；*n.* 减少

用 fall into a decline 开始衰落

例 The consumption of hamburgers and pizza has risen steadily over the 20 year period to 1990 while the consumption of fish and chips has been in decline over that same period with a slight increase in popularity since 1985.
经过20年一直到1990年，汉堡和比萨的消耗量逐渐上升，而同一时期炸鱼和薯条的消耗量呈下降趋势，自1985年又出现缓慢回升。

dip to 下降至……

例 However, while the figures for the Western countries grew to about 15% in around 1990, the figure for Japan dipped to only 2.5% for much of the period.
然而，1990年左右，西方国家的数据上升到15%，而日本在此期间的数据却下降到2.5%。

plunge [plʌndʒ] *vi.* 急剧下降

同 plummet *vi.* 骤然下跌；slump *vi.* 下降

用 plunge to… 猛降到……

例 Finally, the number plunged to only 100 at 4 am. 最后，在4点时数量急剧下降到100。

写作提示

若已有表示急剧下降的动词，不要再加上表示变化幅度的副词，因为它本身就带有decrease dramatically的意思，同理，像soar也一样，本身就表示"突然上涨"的意思。

slump [slʌmp] *vi.* 急剧下降

同 plummet *vi.* 骤然下跌；plunge *vi.*下降，急降

用 slump to… 猛降到……

例 It slumped to 20% in 1940 and rose and fell evenly in the next two decades. 1940年猛降到20%，在接下来的二十年间出现起伏。

表示上升或下降的动词和名词

上升		下降	
动词	名词	动词	名词
increase	an increase of	decrease	a decrease of
rise	a rise of	decline	the decline of
move	movement	fall	a fall of
grow	growth	drop	a drop of
peak	a peak	bottom out	the bottom

fluctuation [ˌflʌktju'eiʃən] *n.* 起伏，波动

拓 fluctuate *vi.* 波动

同 wave *n.* 波动

用 display a fluctuation 呈现波动

a fluctuation in the number of...
在……数量上出现波动

例 In fact there is considerable fluctuation from country to country.
事实上国家间存在着很大的波动。

level off 趋平，呈平稳状态

同 level out 持平；stabilize at 稳定在……

用 level off at … 稳定在……

例 The number levels off at less than 300 people in the following three hours.
接下来的三个小时里，人数稳定在300人以下。

recover [ri'kʌvə] *vi.* 开始上升，恢复

拓 recovery *n.* 恢复

同 regain *vt.* 恢复

例 After this war, the country will take a long time to recover. 经过这场战争，这个国家将需要很长时间才能恢复正常。

develop into 发展成为

同 develop to 发展成……

例 But by 2000 nuclear power, which was not used at all in Australia, had developed into the main resource, producing almost 75% of electricity, at 126 units.
但是到了2000年，在澳大利亚根本就不使用的核能，在（法国）已经发展成为主要的能源来源，占总产量的75%，达到126个单位。

experience [iks'piəriəns] *vt.* 经验，经历

同 witness *vt.* 作为……的见证；作为……发生的地点
undergo *vt.* 经历；see *vt.* 目睹，经历

例 The two decades from 1980 to 2000 experienced a

sharp rise in the number of private cars.
从1980年到2000年期间，私家车的数量呈现快速上升的趋势。

witness ['witnis] *vt.* 见证，作为……见证；作为……发生的地点

用 witness a slight rise in the number of...
在数量上出现缓慢上升
witness a sharp decrease in the amount of...
在数量上出现快速下降

例 It is very clearly witnessed that the percentage of old people in the three countries has been rising at different levels. 可以看出这三个国家老年人的比例已经上升到不同的水平。

unlike [ˌʌn'laik] *prep.* 不像……那样

拓 like *prep.* 像……；likely *adj.* 很可能的

用 unlike A, B is ... 和A不同，B是……

例 According to the line graph, unlike the TV audiences, the number of radio audiences increased rapidly from 6:00 a.m. (4%) to 8:00 a.m., peaking at just over 40%.
如线形图所示，不像电视观众那样，收音机的听众人数从早上6点到8点迅速上升，最高值超过40%。

likely ['laikli] *adj.* 可能的；有希望的；*adv.* 可能

用 be likely to be 可能……

例 Overall the table suggests that households of single adults and those with children were more likely to be living in poverty than those consisting of couples.
总之，该图表展示了和那些只有夫妻两人的家庭相比，单亲家庭和有子女的家庭生活更贫困。

reflect [ri'flekt] *vi.&vt.* 表达，反映

同 mirror *vt.* 反射，反映

用 be reflected in... 在……反映出……

例 This means that a huge amount of water is used in agriculture in Brazil, and this is reflected in the figures for water consumption per person. 这就是说在巴西，大量的水用于农业，这也可以通过人均用水量的数据反映出来。

maintain [mein'tein] *vt.* 保持

同 remain *vi.* 保持

用 maintain the same level 保持同一水平

the number of...remain/maintain steady/stable
数量基本不变

例 Meanwhile, France and Italy generally maintain middle positions, averaging approximately similar spending overall. 与此同时，法国和意大利总体上维持中等水平，接近平均消费水平。

stable ['steibl] *adj.* 稳定的

拓 stabilise *vt.&vi.*（使）稳定；（使）稳固

同 steady *adj.* 稳定的，不变的

constant *adj.* 不变的，恒定的

用 remain stable 保持稳定

例 Although maize remained the least popular food, consumption levels were the most stable. 虽然玉米是最不受欢迎的食物，消耗量却是最稳定的。

constant ['kɔnstənt] *adj.* 始终如一的，恒久不变的

拓 constantly *adv.* 不断地

同 steady *adj.* 稳定的；stable *adj.* 稳定的

unchangeable *adj.* 不变的

用 remain constant 保持不变

例 It is noted that the figure from 1990 to 1995 remained basically constant. 值得注意的是1990年至1995年间的数据基本保持不变。

stand at 达到

同 run at 达到；arrive at 达到

reach *vt.&vi.* 达到；hit *vt.* 达到

例 In 1940 the proportion of people aged 65 or more stood at only 5% in Japan. 1940年，日本人中65岁或以上的人口比例仅达到5%。

变化程度关键词

slight [slait] *adj.* 轻微的，少量的

用 a slight decrease 缓慢的下降

例 The period from 4:00 a.m. to 6:00 a.m. saw another slight rise to 4% in radio listeners. 从早上4点到6点这段时间收音机听众缓慢上升到4%。

substantial [səb'stænʃəl] *adj.* 大量的；实质的

同 dramatic *adj.* 显著的

considerable *adj.* 相当大的

例 We can see immediately that there were substantial differences in the proportion of men and women at different levels. 我们可以很快看出在不同水平上，男性和女性的比例存在很大的差异。

steadily ['stedili] *adv.* 稳定地，稳固地

例 In Great Britain the numbers in prison have increased steadily from 30,000 in 1930 to 80,000 in 1980.
英国监狱的罪犯人数从1930年的30000人逐渐上升到1980年的80000人。

dramatically [drəˈmætikəli] *adv.* 显著地，引人注目地

拓 dramatic *adj.* 戏剧的，引人注目的

同 markedly *adv.* 明显地，显著地

例 Throughout the century, the largest quantity of water was used for agricultural purposes, and this increased dramatically from about 500 km^3 to around 3,000 km^3 in the year 2000. 在这100年间，用水量集中在农业方面，从500立方米迅速上升到2000年的3000立方米。

markedly [ˈmɑːkidli] *adv.* 明显地，显著地，引人注目地

拓 marked *adj.* 显著的

例 On the other hand in Australia, and particularly in New Zealand, the number of people in prisons fell markedly from 1930 to1940. 相反地，在澳大利亚，尤其是新西兰，监狱的罪犯人数从1930年到1940年间迅速下降。

极值描述关键词

peak at 达到峰值

例 After that, the number of new cases increased dramatically, peaking at 1,500 in 1995.（非谓语动词）
此后，新增案件的数量快速上升，在1995年达到最大值1500。
= The number of new cases increased dramatically, reaching the peak at 1,500 in 1995.（名词）
= The number of new cases increased dramatically and peaked at 1,500 in 1995.（并列句，动词）

写作提示

线形图的峰值是图表的重要特征。可用…increase (rise), peaking at…来表达。

peak 也具有名词的词性，因此也有：
reach the peak at…
reach the highest point at…
peak=the highest point （名词）

bottom out at 达到最低值

同 reach the bottom at… 达到最低值
hit the lowest point at… 达到最低值

例 Then, the number of radio listeners declines rapidly, bottom out at 200 at 10:00 a.m..
此后，收音机的听众人数急剧下降，在10点达到最低值200。

写作提示

线形图的谷底是图表的重要特征，可用非谓语动词形式…decrease (fall), bottoming out at…来表述。

zenith ['zeniθ] *n.* 顶点，极点

同 summit *n.* 顶点；top *n.* 顶点；pinnacle *n.* 极点
peak *n.* 最高点，顶点

用 reach the zenith of… 达到最高点
at the zenith of… 在最高点

例 The number of the people reaches its zenith at the subway at 8:00 a.m..
早上八点地铁里的人数最多。

nadir ['neidiə] *n.* 最低限度

同 the lowest point 最小值；bottom *n.* 最低点

用 reach one's nadir 达到最低点

例 Household goods was changing dramatically with the nadir in 1977 and the zenith in 1996.
家庭用品变化很大，在1977年达到最低值，在1996年达到最高值。

对比描述关键词

overtake [ˌəuvəˈteik] *vt.&vi.* 超出

同 exceed *vt.* 超过

用 be overtaken by… 被……超过

例 The consumption of chicken, on the other hand, showed an upward trend, overtaking that of lamb in 1980 and that of beef in 1989.
相反地，鸡肉的消耗量呈上升的趋势，均超过了1980年羊肉和1989年牛肉的消耗量。

写作提示

线形图的交叉点是图表的重要特征，一定要体现出来，常用的词有overtake/outnumber/exceed/surpass。在用这些词的时候，后面常常接that of…。

outnumber [autˈnʌmbə] *vt.* 数量多于，比……多

用 A outnumbers that of B A的量超过B的量

例 At the higher levels education, men with postgraduate diplomas clearly outnumbered their female counterparts.
从高学历角度看，拥有硕士学历的男性比例超过了女性。

exceed [ikˈsiːd] *vt.&vi.* 超过，超越，（在数量和质量等方面）胜过

例 The proportion of women students exceeded that of men students in this level.
这一水平的女生比例要超出男生。

surpass [səˈpɑːs] *vt.* 胜过，超过；优于；多于

例 The proportion of women students in higher education surpassed that of men students.

接受高等教育的女性比例超过男性。

compare [kəm'peə] *vt.&vi.* 比较，对照

拓 comparison *n.* 比较

comparative *adj.* 比较的，相当的

例 The charts compare the sources of electricity in Australia and France in the years 1980 and 2000.

这几个图表对从1980年到2004年间，澳大利亚和法国的电力来源进行了比较。

contrast [kən'trɑːst] *vi.&vt.* 对比；差异，差别

例 The table illustrates the differences in agricultural consumption in some areas of the world by contrasting the amount of irrigated land in Brazil (26,500 km^2) with that in D.R.C (100km^2).

该表格通过将巴西（26500 km^2）和刚果(100km^2)的灌溉面积进行对比，展示了在世界某些地区农业用水量的不同。

in contrast 相对比而言

同 by contrast 相对比而言

用 in marked contrast to 呈明显的对比

in a sharp contrast to 呈明显的对比

例 In contrast, more women held undergraduate diplomas (70%) and marginally more women reached the degree level (55%).

相对比而言，只有稍微多一些的女性拥有学位(55%)，更多的女性拥有大学文凭(70%)。

while [hwail] *conj.* 然而

同 whereas *conj.* 然而；whilst *conj.* 然而

例 From 1950 onwards, industrial water use grew steadily to just over 1,000 km^3, while domestic water use rose more slowly to only 300 km^3, both far below the levels of consumption by agriculture. 从1950年开始，工业用水稳步增长到超过1000立方米，而家庭用水增长缓慢，仅仅上升到300立方米，二者均远远低于农业方面的用水量。

写作提示

while一词出现的频率很高，在具体使用中，前后连接两个句子，且其变化趋势是相反的。几乎篇篇真题范文中都会出现。

on the other hand 相反地

同 conversely *adv.* 相反地；on the contrary 相反地

by contrast 相比之下

例 The consumption of chicken, on the other hand, showed an upward trend.

然而，鸡肉的消耗量却呈现上升趋势。

match [mætʃ] *vt.&vi.* （使）相配，（使）相称

用 be matched by 和……相匹配

例 In contrast, France used coal as a source for only 25 units of electricity in 1980, which was matched by natural gas.

相反，在1980年法国的电力只有25%来源于煤炭，和天然气所占的比例不相上下。

the same can be said about... 与……相同

同 this is true of... 符合于……

so does... ……也是

be the same as... 与……一样

例 The consumption of water is on the rise, and the same can be said about the food consumption in these three countries.

在这三个国家中，水的消耗量呈上升趋势，食物的消耗量也是如此。

not so...as 不像……那么……

例 The consumption of fish also declined, but not so dramatic as beef.
鱼肉的消耗量也在下降，但下降幅度没有牛肉那么大。

also... but... 也……但是……

例 Water used in the industrial and domestic sectors also increased, but consumption was minimal until mid-century.
工业和家庭用水也有所上升，但到中世纪中期其消耗量还是很少。

at odds with 与……不一致

同 be opposite to 与……相反

例 The drop in 1995 was at odds with the sharp rise in 1999.
1995年的下降状况与1999年的明显上涨趋势相反。

neck and neck 并驾齐驱，不分上下

例 The two countries stand neck and neck on both levels of education and show slight differences in terms of genders.
两个国家在教育层次上不分上下，就性别而言，没有很大的不同。

counterpart ['kauntəpɑ:t] *n.* 相对应的人或物

例 While the number of full-time female workers grew, that of full-time male counterpart declined.
全职女性员工的人数上升，而全职男性员工的人数下降。

写作提示

对比描述的句子中，前文提到的名词可以用counterpart代替。

corresponding [ˌkɔrisˈpɔndiŋ] *adj.* 相当的，对应的，相关的

用 corresponding quantity 相应的数量
the corresponding period last year 去年同期

例 Corresponding figures for this item were 27 and 48.
这一项目的相关数字为27和48。

previous [ˈpriːviəs] *adj.* 先前的，以前的

拓 previously *adv.* 先前；以前

同 former *adj.* 从前的，前者的
earlier *adj.* 早先的，早期的
preceding *adj.* 前面的
prior *adj.* 在前的

用 over the previous year 前一年
previous to 在……之前

例 In 2006, the total population of Japan stood at 127.77 million, remaining at basically the same level as the previous year.
2006年，日本的人口总数达到了12777万，与前一年的人口总数基本持平。

former [ˈfɔːmə] *adj.*（两者中）前者的

反 latter *adj.* 后者的

用 the former…, the latter…
前者……，后者……

例 The former pie chart shows how the water was used in the city and the latter one gives information about the water consumption in agriculture.

前一个饼图描述了该城市的用水情况，后一个饼图描述了在农业方面水的消耗量。

similar ['similə] *adj.* 类似的，同类的，相似的

拓 similarly *adv.* 同样地，类似于

similarity *n.* 类似，相似点

dissimilar *adj.* 不同的

同 alike *adj.* 相似的

用 be similar to… 与……相似

例 It is thought that the proportion of elderly people will be similar in the three countries.

三个国家的老龄化人口的比例接近。

parallel ['pærəlel] *vt.* 与……平行，与……相当

同 equal *vt.* 与……相等或相同

keep pace with 与……保持同步

parallelise *vt.* 与……平行

用 This can be paralleled with… 与……平行

例 This was almost paralleled with the trend of fish and chicken. 这一趋势与鱼和鸡肉的变化相同。

comparatively [kəm'pærətivli] *adv.* 对比地，相对地

拓 comparative *adj.* 比较的，相对的

同 relatively *adv.* 相当地，相对地

例 The number of people begins to decline steadily to a comparatively low level.

人数开始稳步下降到相对较低的水平。

relatively ['relətivli] *adv.* 相对地，比较而言，相当

拓 relative *adj.* 相对的；relation *n.* 关系

例 The number remains relatively low in summer compared with the winter.

和冬天相比，夏天的数量相对小一些。

conversely [kən'və:sli] *adv.* 相反地，颠倒地

拓 converse *adj.* 相反的

同 contrarily *adv.* 相反地

inversely *adv.* 相反地

例 In the future, the rate of aging will continue to rise while conversely the rate of the working generation will decrease. 未来，老龄化的比率将会持续上升，而上班族比率将会下降。

dominance ['dɔminəns] *n.* 优势；支配地位

拓 dominant *adj.* 占优势的

同 predominance *n.* 优势

leading position 首要地位

用 the dominance of… ……的主导

例 Thc new source of energy, especially nuclear was on the rise while the traditional ones, though it's still the dominant.
尽管传统的能源仍然占主导地位，新型能源，尤其是核能，呈上升的趋势。

overwhelmingly [ˌəuvə'welmiŋli] *adv.* 占压倒性优势地，势不可挡地

拓 overwhelming *adj.* 压倒性的，势不可挡的

overwhelm *vt.* 压倒

用 overwhelmingly greater than 超出……很多

例 These figures in 1999 were overwhelmingly greater than the corresponding figure in 2009.
1999年的数据要比2009年的数据多很多。

evenly ['i:vənli] *adv.* 平滑地；有规律地；均匀地；相等地

拓 even *adj.* 有规律的；均匀的；相等的

同 identically *adv.* 同一地，相等地

equally *adv.* 同样地，相等地

例 They were evenly matched in the aspect.
他们在这一方面旗鼓相当。

differ ['difə] *vi.* 不同

拓 difference *n.* 不同
different *adj.* 不同的
differentiate *vt.&vi.* 区分，区别

用 differ from… 与……不同

例 As is displayed in the table, the figure of underground railway systems including date opened, kilometers of route and passengers per year in six cities differed.
如表格所示，在六个城市中，每年的地铁系统信息如开始日期、路线长度及乘客等各不相同。

prevail [pri'veil] *vi.* 占优势

拓 prevalence *n.* 流行，普遍
prevailing *adj.* 流行的

用 prevail over 优胜于……
prevail against sb. 胜过某人

例 The use of public transport still prevails among the students.
乘坐公共交通在学生中仍然十分盛行。

majority [mə'dʒɔːriti] *n.* 多数，大多数

反 minority *n.* 少数，小部分

用 be in the majority 占大多数
overwhelming majority 压倒性的多数

例 The majority of people choose to go to work by public transport.
大多数人上班选择乘坐公共交通工具。

major ['meidʒə] *adj.* 主要的

用 play a major part 起着重要的作用

例 Food always play a major part in the average family expenditure in Britain.
在英国，食物在家庭平均支出中占主要部分。

minority [mai'nɔriti] *n.* 少数，小部分

拓 minor *adj.* 较小的

反 majority *n.* 多数

用 in the minority 占少数的

be in a minority of one 得不到任何人的支持

例 Only a minority of British households do not have a car.
英国只有少数家庭没有汽车。

percent [pə'sent] *n.* 百分比

拓 percentage *n.* 百分比，百分率

例 I agree with you a hundred percent.
我百分之百地同意你的看法。

times [taimz] *n.* 倍数

例 The production has increased by five times since 1999. 自1999年以来，产量增加到原来的5倍。

double ['dʌbl] *vt.&vi.*（使）加倍；*adv.* 两倍地，双重地

同 twice *adv.* 两次，两倍

例 Between these years electricity production almost doubled, rising from 100 units to 170 units in Australia, and from 90 to 180 units in France. 在这些年间，电产量几乎翻倍，澳大利亚从100单位上升到170单位，而法国从90单位上升到180单位。

marginally ['mɑ:dʒinəli] *adv.* 少量地，最低限度地

拓 marginal *adj.* 微小的；少量的

例 Italy's spending on personal stereos is only marginally greater than that of France, while spending on toys is equal between the two.

意大利在随身听上的花销刚刚超过法国，而在玩具上的花销两国相当。

considerably [kən'sidərəbəli] *adv.* 相当地，非常地

拓 considerable *adj.* 相当大的

例 The chart shows that high income earners consumed considerably more fast foods than the other income groups. 该图表显示出高收入群体在快餐上的花费要比其他群体多得多。

minimal ['miniməl] *adj.* 最小的，极少的

反 maximal *adj.* 最大的

例 Fortunately, the storm only did minimal damage to the farmer's crops. 很幸运，暴风雨只使农民的庄稼受到轻微的损害。

by far ……得多，更，尤其

用 …by far the most popular of/among…, with…
……是最受欢迎的，数量达到……

例 In 1979 beef was by far the most popular of these foods, with about 225 grams consumed per person per week. 在1979年，牛肉最受欢迎，每人每周食用量达到大约225克。

写作提示

对比数据的词汇，放在形容词最高级的前面，如by far the most…。

favour ['feivə] *vt.* 赞成；喜爱

拓 favourable *adj.* 有利的
favourably *adv.* 有利地

用 the trend favours A rather than B
倾向于A而不是B

例 Average income earners also favored hamburgers, spending 33 pence per person per week, followed by fish and chips at 24 pence, then pizza at 11 pence.
均等收入的家庭也很青睐汉堡，人均每周在汉堡上的花销是33便士，在炸鱼和薯条上的花销量是24便士，在比萨上的花销量是11便士。

leading ['li:diŋ] *adj.* 主要的

用 the leading position 首要地位

例 Generally speaking, educational levels in both age groups in Europe are in leading positions.
一般来说，欧洲这两个年龄段的教育水平处于领先地位。

rank [ræŋk] *vt.&vi.* 占……地位，列为

用 rank the second 排名第二
rank the first 排名第一
rank the highest 位列最高

例 In 1999, Australia ranked the second, behind the USA.
1999年，澳大利亚排名第二，位于美国之后。

turn out to be 结果是，原来是

用 …ranks first, while…turns out to be the lowest.
……排名第一，而……最低。

例 According to the pie charts, nuclear power ranked the highest as the sources of electricity, while natural gas turned out to be the lowest in 2000.
如饼图所示，在2000年核能是电能的主要来源，结果天然气是占比例最小的能源。

followed by 接下来是……

例 Fish and chips remain the most popular fast food, followed by hamburgers and then pizza.

炸鱼和薯条是最受欢迎的快餐，接下来是汉堡，然后是比萨。

significant [sig'nifikənt] *adj.* 重要的

拓 significantly *adv.* 显著地
significance *n.* 意义，重要性

反 insignificant *adj.* 不重要的；无意义的

例 Police believed it was significant that he had recently opened a bank account abroad.
警方认为，他最近在国外银行新开账户的事很重要。

为了更真实、更权威地反映雅思作文真题，本单元还列举了最新的雅思作文真题并链接相关的机经关键词，从而使考生将所学的词汇更直接地、更有效地应用在考试中。

链接机经关键词

- **图表类型**

线形图/曲线图(Line/Curve Graph)
柱状图(Bar Chart/Column)
饼状图(Pie Chart)
表　格(Table)
流程图或地图(Process Diagram/Flow Chart, Map)

- **开头段转述题干**

给出信息(give/offer/provide/information)
比例与比率(percentage/proportion/ratio)
不同水平(the different levels)

数据(data/figure/statistic/number)
人口的信息(information about the population)
电力来源(the source of the electricity)
用水量(the amount of water)

如图所示

according to.../as shown in.../as can be seen from...
It is clear from the figures/statistics...
It is noted that...

变化趋势及举出具体数值

上升(be on the upward trend/show an upward movement/be on the rise)
下降(decline/fall/drop/sink/dip/decrease/descend)
急剧下降(plummet/plunge)
下降(be on a declining trend/be on the decline/show a downward trend)
引出具体数值(particularly/to be specific/specifically/to be more exact/more exactly)
达到(stand at/run at/arrive at/reach/amount to/hit/come to)
呈平稳状态(level off at/level out at/hover at/stabilize at/reach a plateau at)
达到极值(peak at/bottom out at)

对比与比较

与……相似(be similar to...)
不像……那么(not so ... as)
然而(while/however/whereas)
与此相反(in contrast/by contrast/on the other hand/on the contrary/conversely)
A是B的几倍(A is ...times as much/many as B)

2 G类书信词汇

感谢信

考点回顾

20121103 感谢曾经的同事
20100626 感谢老师

express [iks'pres] *vt.* 表达

用 express one's gratitude for… 表示感谢
express one's thanks for… 表示感谢
express one's appreciation for... 表示感谢

例 I am writing to express my thanks for what you did on the party yesterday. 给您写信是想对您在昨天晚会上的帮助表示感谢。

convey [kən'vei] *vt.* 传达，转达，表达

同 express *vt.* 表达
show *vt.* 显示

用 convey one's heartfelt thanks to sb. for…
因某事向某人表达最衷心的感谢

例 I would like to convey in this letter my heartfelt thanks to you for your patience and help.
我想对您的耐心和帮助表示衷心的感谢。

sincerely [sin'siəli] *adv.* 真诚地，由衷地，诚恳地

拓 sincere *adj.* 真诚的，诚挚的
sincerity *n.* 真实，诚挚

例 I sincerely hope that you can consider this matter seriously. 我真诚地希望您能认真地考虑此事。

gratitude ['grætitju:d] *n.* 感谢，感激

拓 grateful *adj.* 感谢的

用 express one's gratitude 表示感激

例 I am writing to express my gratitude for you and I really appreciate the help that you have given to me. 给您写信是为了向您表达我的感谢，真心地谢谢您为我所做的一切。

extend [iks'tend] *vt.* 延伸，扩大；提供，给予，发出（邀请、欢迎等）

用 extend one's thanks 表示感谢
extend cordial welcome 表示热忱欢迎
extend our sincere congratulations on 表示衷心祝贺

例 I am writing to you to extend my thanks for your timely help. 对您及时的帮助，我非常感谢。

写作提示

在邀请信中，也可以用extend引导的短语来表达欢迎，如：

I would like to extend my warmest/cordial welcome to all of you. 请允许我向各位贵宾表示热烈的欢迎。

appreciate [ə'pri:ʃieit] *vt.* 欣赏，感激

拓 appreciated *adj.* 欣赏的，感激的
appreciation *n.* 欣赏，感谢

同 be grateful 感激
express appreciation 表达感激

例 Anyway, I would like to appreciate what you will do for me.
不管怎么说，我很感激您为我做的事情。

写作提示

基本上所有信件的结尾都要有一句期盼回复：look forward to the reply。

一句感谢的话：appreciate for what you have done for me。

kindness ['kaindnis] *n.* 友好的态度，好心

同 warm-heartedness *n.* 好心
hospitality *n.* 好客，殷勤；geniality *n.* 亲切

例 How can I reward you for your kindness?
我怎样才能报答你的好意呢?

generosity [ˌdʒenə'rɔsiti] *n.* 慷慨，大方，宽容

拓 generous *adj.* 慷慨的，大方的

同 unselfishness *n.* 不自私，慷慨

反 stinginess *n.* 小气

例 We were completely knocked out by their generosity.
他们的宽宏大量使我们感到十分吃惊。

hospitality [ˌhɔspi'tæliti] *n.* 友好款待，热情招待

拓 hospitable *adj.* 热情友好的

同 kindness *n.* 仁慈，好意
warmth *n.* 温暖，热情

例 Many thanks for your kindness and hospitality.
非常感谢你的盛情款待。

heartfelt ['hɑ:tfelt] *adj.* 衷心的，真诚的

同 from the bottom of one's heart 内心深处的

用 one's heartfelt thanks 由衷的感谢

例 I would like to express in this letter my heartfelt thanks to you for taking good care of my child.
给您写信是为了表达我对您衷心的感谢，谢谢您照顾我的孩子。

写作提示

当衷心的感谢用 heartfelt 或sincere 都无法表达时，可以用下面的英文：

I wish there were a better word than "thank you" to express my appreciation for your generous help.

My appreciation to you for your kindness is beyond description.

I really don't know how to thank you enough for your help.

cordial ['kɔːdjəl] *adj.* 热忱的，诚恳的

拓 cordiality *n.* 热诚，真挚

同 amiable *adj.* 和蔼可亲的，亲切的

用 cordial thanks 真诚的感谢

cordial hospitality 盛情接待

cordial feeling 亲切感

例 Please accept my cordial thanks for your timely help.

对您及时的帮助，请接受我衷心的感谢。

beyond words 难以言表，无法用语言表达

同 beyond description 难以形容

例 My true gratitude is beyond the words.

无法用语言表达我真挚的谢意。

considerate [kən'sidərit] *adj.* 体谅的，考虑周到的，体贴的

拓 considerateness *n.* 体谅

considerately *adv.* 体谅地

同 thoughtful *adj.* 体贴的，关切的

用 considerate service 周到的服务

be considerate of 体贴的，细心的

例 I am deeply impressed by considerate service in the hotel.

对于宾馆无微不至的服务，我印象深刻。

render ['rendə] *vt.* 提供（帮助等），给予（服务等）

同 provide *vt.* 提供； *vt.* 提供

例 I would like to take this opportunity to express my deep appreciation for the kind assistance you rendered me.
借此机会对您给予我的帮助，深表谢意。

assistance [ə'sistəns] *n.* 援助，帮助

同 aid *n.* 援助；favour *n.* 帮助；help *n.* 帮助

用 be of assistance 有好处，有用处
come to one's assistance 来帮忙
go to one's assistance 去帮忙

例 Your guide will be of assistance to my work.
您的指导会对我的工作有所帮助。

indebted [in'detid] *adj.* 感激的

用 be (feel) indebted to sb. 对某人感激的

例 I feel deeply indebted to you. 我对您不胜感激。

repay [riː'pei] *vt.* 报答，回报

同 return *vt.* 返回，报答
reciprocate *vt.* 报答
pay back *vt.* 偿还，报答

用 repay one's kindness 回报谢意

例 I wish I could repay you somehow when the opportunity arises.
但愿我能以某种方式回报你。

写作提示

结尾再次表示感谢，通常加上again/once more。例：
I must thank you again for your generous help.
Again, I would like to express my sincere thanks to you.
Thank you again for your kindness.
Thank you for what you have done again.

投诉信

考点回顾

20120901 投诉机场
20100320 投诉旅游公司
20100123 投诉电信公司

attention [ə'tenʃən] *n.* 专心，留心，注意

用 draw (attract) sb.'s attention 引起某人的注意
bring sth. to sb.'s attention 使某人注意某事
catch (arrest) sb.'s attention 引起某人注目
focus (center) one's attention on…
把注意力集中在……上
give one's attention to… 注意
pay attention to… 注意

例 I hope you will give due attention to this matter.
我希望您能对此事给予足够的重视。

写作提示

信件的开头，一般可以用draw sb.'s attention来让收信人关注一下某个问题。信件的结尾可以表达希望收信人能对某个问题，如家具、维修、服务等投诉的问题给予关注。

如投诉餐馆噪音大：

I am writing to draw your attention that the noise in your restaurant is so loud and interrupts our normal life.

如写信投诉租住公寓：

There are some problems with the flat that I wish to bring to attention.

complain [kəm'plein] *vi.&vt.* 抱怨，诉苦；投诉

拓 complaint *n.* 投诉

用 complain about sth. 抱怨，投诉

complain of 抱怨，诉苦

complain to 向……抱怨

例 I am writing to complain about some of the furniture.

我写信是反映一下家具的问题。

disappoint [ˌdisə'pɔint] *vt.* 使失望

拓 disappointment *n.* 失望，沮丧

disappointing *adj.* 令人失望的

用 be disappointed with… 对……感到失望

例 I'm sorry to disappoint your expectation.

很遗憾，我辜负了您的期望。

satisfy ['sætisfai] *vi.&vt.* 使满意，满足

拓 satisfied *adj.* 满意的

satisfactory *adj.* 令人满意的

satisfaction *n.* 满意，满足

用 satisfy the people's needs 满足人民需求

例 I am not satisfied with the service in the hotel, for I often get into the trouble when I use the hot water.

我对宾馆的服务很不满意，用热水的时候经常遇到麻烦。

写作提示

对……不满的表达法

be disappointed with sth.和be unsatisfied with sth.可以表达出对服务、设施等的不满，没有达到预期的设想（disappoint your expectation），也可以用sth. is disappointing或 The service is unsatisfactory。

express one's dissatisfaction with... 表示对……的不满

同 express one's discomfort with...
表示对……的不满

例 I am writing to you to express my dissatisfaction with the noise caused by the dogs in the community.
我给您写信主要想表达对社区里的狗产生噪音的不满。

写作提示

投诉信里表达不满常用express one's discomfort，感谢信里表达感激常用express one's gratitude。

结尾句可以加上I could not be more satisfied if you can kindly...（如果您能……，我将会非常满意）提出解决的建议。

put up with 忍受，容忍

同 bear *vt.* 忍受
tolerate *vt.* 忍受

用 I can hardly put up with...any more.
我再也忍受不了……

例 I cannot put up with my noisy roommates any more.
我再也忍受不了吵闹的室友了。

deal with 处理，安排

同 handle *vt.* 处理
take measures 采取措施
resolve *vt.* 解决
address *vt.* 解决

用 deal with sth. as soon as possible 尽快处理某事

例 I would really like to deal with this matter as soon as possible. 我很希望此事能尽快解决。

写作提示

在表达希望尽快采取有效的措施时，我们还可用take efficient measures 或者 take immediate/prompt measures；as soon as possible "尽快"，表达一种强烈的愿望。

accommodation [əˌkɔməˈdeiʃən] *n.* 住宿，食宿

拓 accommodate *vt.* 提供住宿；使适应

例 I would like to work in Shanghai if the company provides accommodation.
如果公司能提供住宿，我愿意到上海工作。

as you may remember 您应该还记得

同 as you know 如您所知
as you may guess 如您所知

例 As you may remember, the dining table is in very poor condition and has uneven legs. 您应该还记得，餐桌已经很破旧了，桌腿也不稳。

as you know 如你所知

例 As you know, we'll be moving to a new house soon and there are a few things that I won't be able to take with me. 如你所知，我很快就要搬进新家了，有几样东西我不能带过去。

arrangement [əˈreindʒmənt] *n.* 安排；协议；约定

拓 arrange *vt.&vi.* 安排

用 come to an arrangement 谈妥，达成协议
make arrangements for 为……做出安排

例 The local newspaper made arrangements for an interview with professor Stein.
当地报纸安排对斯坦教授进行专访。

concern [kən'sə:n] *n.* 关心，关系，关心的事；*vt.* 涉及，关系到

用 as far as…be concerned 就……而言

be concerned about (for) 关心，担忧，挂念

be concerned in (with) 与……有关系

例 This matter concerns all of us.

这件事与我们每个人都有关系。

repair [ri'peə] *vi.&vt.* 修复，修理；*n.* 修理，修补，维修工作

用 beyond repair 无法修理

in bad repair 破损的，失修的

in good repair 修理得很好的

out of repair 失修，破损

under repair 在修理中

例 My bicycle has to be repaired.

我的自行车需要修一修。

写作提示

提醒房东该修理一些家具，并不是要房东本人来维修，而是要他找人维修，就用have sth. done 的形式，如have the oven repaired（找人修理灶具）。

make up for 补偿，弥补

同 compensate *vt.&vi.* 补偿，赔偿

remedy *vt.* 补救；*n.* 治疗；补救

用 make up for the loss 弥补损失

例 How can we make up to you for what you've suffered?

我们如何能够补偿您所遭受的损害?

refund ['ri:fʌnd] *vi.&.vt.* 退还，偿还；*n.* 偿还，退款

拓 refundable *adj.* 可偿还的，可退还的

同 repay *vt.&vi.* 偿还，报答；pay back 偿还

例 After a few days' delay, the shop refunded my money at last. 经过几天的拖延，这家商店最终还是将钱退给了我。

recurrence [ri'kʌrəns] *n.* 循环，再发生

同 repetition *n.* 重复

用 prevent the recurrence 避免再次发生

例 You should make great effort to prevent the recurrence of mailing the telephone bill to the wrong place.
你们应该尽量避免再次发生电话账单寄错的事件。

look forward to 盼望，期待

例 I look forward to hearing from you.
期望得到您的回复。

写作提示

look forward to在真题范文中也常用，我们也别忘了在信件的结尾加上一句：look forward to（介词to后面加名词或者动名词）。

如：I am looking forward to your reply.
I am looking forward to seeing you.

convenient [kən'viːnjənt] *adj.* 方便的，便利的

同 available *adj.* 可利用的；suitable *adj.* 适当的

反 inconvenient *adj.* 不便的，打扰的

例 May I come and talk with you whenever it's convenient?
在你方便时我能来和你谈谈吗?

写作提示

提出问题的解决办法时可以这样表达：If it is more convenient for you, perhaps you could simply… 如果方便的话，或许您可以……

这样既提出了建议，也不失礼貌，何乐而不为呢?

at your earliest convenience 在您方便时请早日……

例 I am looking forward to a favorable response at your earliest convenience. 期待您尽早地回复。

furniture ['fəːnitʃə] *n.* 家具

同 furnishings *n.* 家具；供应；equipment *n.* 设备

用 a piece of furniture 一件家具

例 The new house is a bit smaller so I have to sell some furniture and I was wondering if you might be interested. 新房子要小得多，所以我要卖掉一些家具，我想知道你对此有兴趣么？

写作提示

真题范文中对furniture的投诉：

As you may remember, the dining table is in very poor condition and has uneven legs. It also does not match the dining chairs as these are too low to be comfortable for a table of that height.

链接机经关键词

投诉或抱怨的事情

- can't put up with/can't bear（不能忍受）the awful service（糟糕的服务）and bad manners（不礼貌），unprofessional service and attitude（不专业的服务和态度）
- the noise caused by the dogs in the neighborhood（社区里狗叫声）is inconceivable
- the bad sanitary situation in the restaurant（宾馆饭店的卫生条件）is a disturbance（干扰）and

nuisance（麻烦事）for the residents（居民）

- 家具问题：the furniture discomforts me

⊙ 你对解决问题的建议

- investigate（调查）this matter（事件）and take some effective and prompt measures
- change a new product, otherwise, I would ask you to give the money back
- the authorities concerned consider（相关部门、当局）the suggestions and improve the situation
- make up for the loss（弥补损失）, deliver the right thing or refund（退款）me
- consider this matter seriously and make an effort to prevent the recurrence of this kind（防止类似事件发生）

⊙ 期盼得到回复

- look forward to the reply

道歉信

考点回顾

20100220 向老师道歉

20091008 向朋友道歉

apologise [ə'pɔlədʒaiz] *vi.&vt.* 道歉

拓 apology *n.* 道歉

用 apologise for... 因……而道歉

apologise for oneself 为自己辩解

例 The US has apologised to Britain for the accident.

美国已就这次意外事故向英国致歉。

spoil [spɔil] *vt.* 破坏，毁坏，毁掉

拓 spoiled *adj.* 被宠坏的

spoilt *adj.* 宠坏的；损坏的

同 destroy *vt.* 毁坏，破坏；ruin *vt.* 毁灭

例 I was very shocked to get your letter saying that the noise from my flat has been spoiling your evenings and causing you some distress.

您信上说我公寓里发出的噪音在夜里干扰了您的休息并给您带来烦恼，对此我很吃惊。

disturb [dis'tə:b] *vt.&vi.* 打扰，妨碍

拓 disturbing *adj.* 烦扰的，令人不安的

disturbance *n.* 干扰，骚乱

同 annoy *vt.* 骚扰；*vi.* 令人讨厌

bother *vt.&vi.* 烦扰，打扰；interrupt *vt.&vi.* 打断

例 He'll work only during daytime hours, so you won't be disturbed in the evenings again, I promise.

他会在白天工作，所以我保证晚上再不会打扰您了。

guilty ['gilti] *adj.* 有罪的，内疚的

拓 guilt *n.* 内疚；guiltless *adj.* 无罪的

同 blameworthy *adj.* 应受谴责的

例 I feel very guilty for forgetting the appointment.

忘记了约会我感到非常内疚。

assure [ə'ʃuə] *vt.* 保证，担保，使确信

拓 assurance *n.* 保证，断言

同 guarantee *vt.* 保证

convince *vt.* 使确信

make certain 确信

用 assure sb. that… 向……保证

例 I assure you that the problem will never happen again. 我向您保证类似的事情不会再发生。

写作提示

在道歉信里，除了态度要诚恳，还要提出解决措施，最后使别人感到信服。如：I assured you that everything would turn out all right.

promise ['prɔmis] *n.* 承诺，诺言；*vt.&vi.* 允诺，答应

同 keep one's word 允诺，答应

用 give a promise=make a promise 许诺

keep one's promise 遵守诺言

break one's promise 违背诺言

例 They promised that the work would all be finished by next week. 他们保证到下星期完成全部工作。

excuse sb. for… 原谅

例 I hope you will excuse me for my carelessness.

我希望您能原谅我的粗心大意。

careless ['keələs] *adj.* 粗心的，草率的，疏忽的

拓 carelessness *n.* 粗心大意

care *n.* 关怀，照料

careful *adj.* 仔细的

同 thoughtless *adj.* 欠考虑的，考虑不周的

inconsiderate *adj.* 粗心的

例 Any careless may result in a terrible consequence.

一丁点儿的粗心都能引起严重的后果。

negligent ['neglidʒənt] *adj.* 疏忽的，粗心大意的

反 careful *adj.* 仔细的

thoughtful *adj.*体贴的，关切的

cautious *adj.* 谨慎的，十分小心的

例 How negligent I am to forget such an important matter!

我可真粗心呀，竟然忘记了这么重要的事。

unthoughtful [ˌʌn'θɔːtful] *adj.* 考虑不周的，粗心的，轻率的

反 thoughtful *adj.* 深思的，体贴的

例 I feel terribly sorry for my unthoughtful behaviour.
我为自己鲁莽的行为道歉。

overlook [ˌəuvə'luk] *vt.* 忽视，忽略

同 neglect *vt.* 疏忽，忽视
disregard *vt.* 忽视，不理
ignore *vt.* 忽视

例 The important details were overlooked by them.
很重要的细节都被他们忽略掉了。

neglect [ni'glekt] *vt.* 疏忽，忽视；*n.* 忽略，疏忽

拓 neglected *adj.* 被忽视的
neglectful *adj.* 疏忽的
negligence *n.* 粗心大意，忽视
negligent *adj.* 疏忽的，粗心大意的

例 It might compensate in some way for his seeming neglect of her.
这样也许会稍许弥补一下他在表面上对她的忽视。

regret [ri'gret] *vt.&vi.* 懊悔，惋惜，遗憾

拓 regretful *adj.* 后悔的，遗憾的
regrettable *adj.* 令人遗憾的
regretless *adj.* 无悔的，没有遗憾的

用 regret doing sth. 对做过的事表示遗憾
regret to do sth. 对要做的事遗憾

例 I now regret saying what I said.
现在我为自己说过的话感到后悔。

链接机经关键词

◉ 道歉的事件(events)

- 别人带来的不便 (inconveniences)
  没能按时赴约(can't keep the appointment)
  房屋装修产生的噪音(the noise caused by the decoration)
  修理东西产生的噪音(the noise caused by the repair work)
  不小心摔坏别人的东西(break something)
  不得不拒绝别人的邀请(have to decline/turn down other's offer or invitation)
- 表示道歉 (apology and regret) 及事件缘由(reasons):
  不知道你为此忍受了这么多(I had no idea that you would be able to hear so much)
- 何如解决(how to deal with it)
  找来专业的建筑人员来完成此项目(call in a professional builder to finish the work)
  找个时间来碰一下头(find another time to have a get-together)

询问信

考点回顾

20100109 询问大学的课程
20090711 询问住宿情况

inquiry [in'kwaiəri] *n.* 询问
拓 inquire *vt.&vi.* 询问

用 make inquiry 询问，打听

例 Your prompt and favorable attention to my inquiry would be highly appreciated.
对您及时地回答我的问题，我深表谢意。

seek [siːk] *vt.&vi.* 寻找，探索

同 look for 寻找

用 seek after 追求，探索
seek out 找出
seek for personal development 追求个人发展

例 I would like to seek the information about the accommodation fee in your university.
我想知道学校关于住宿费的信息。

obtain [əb'tein] *vt.&vi.* 获得

拓 obtainable *adj.* 能得到的

同 gain *vt.&vi.* 获得

用 obtain some information about…
获取关于……的信息

例 I would like to obtain some information about the tuition fee.
我想知道关于学费的信息。

hope [həup] *n.* 希望

拓 hopeful *adj.* 有希望的
hopeless *adj.* 绝望的

用 lay one's hope in 寄希望于……

例 I am writing to you in the hope that I may obtain the detailed information about the part-time job in the campus. 给您写信希望能获得关于校园内兼职工作的详细信息。

wonder ['wʌndə] *vi.* 想知道

用 wonder if 想知道是否

wonder whether 想知道是否

例 I wondered if there is a tennis club available.

我想知道是否有一个网球俱乐部。

写作提示

wonder表示“不知道，想知道”的意思时，通常都用下面两种方式提问。I wondered if…，I was wondering if…

注意啦，wonder一词多用于过去式wondered或是过去进行时was wondering的形式，为什么呢？仔细想想，你在和别人说“我想知道……”的时候，你的大脑已经有这个问题，思考过了，所以应用过去的时态。

provide [prə'vaid] *vt.&vi.* 提供

同 offer *vt.* 提供

用 provide sb. with sth. 为某人提供某物

provide sb. with information about…

为某人提供关于……的信息

例 I am writing to see if it is possible for you to provide me with information about the course next term.

给您写信，想知道是否可以提供给我有关下学期课程的相关信息。

inform [in'fɔːm] *vt.* 通知，告诉

拓 information *n.* 信息

informative *adj.* 见闻广博的

同 notify *vt.* 通告，通知

用 inform sb. of sth. 通知某人某事

例 If there is any information about the sports club, please inform me promptly. 如果有关于体育俱乐部的相关信息，请及时通知我。

detailed ['di:teild] *adj.* 详细的

用 detailed information about… 关于……的详情

例 I would like some detailed information about the selected courses.

我想知道关于选修课的详细信息。

be concerned about 对……关心

同 care about 关心

例 I am greatly concerned about the clubs in the community.

我很想知道社区俱乐部的信息。

reply [ri'plai] *vi.&vt.* 回答，答复；*n.* 回答，答复

同 response *n.* 响应，反应

用 reply to sb. 回复某人

例 I am looking forward to a favorable reply at your earliest convenience.

期望您尽早给予答复。

链接机经关键词

⊙ **询问的事由**

- 首先是你的个人信息(personal information)。
- 课程(I am writing to seek information about course)、学费(tuition fee)、住宿安排(accommodation)、入学考试(the entrance to the university)和俱乐部(club)等等。希望能够提供进一步的信息(provide with the further information)。

⊙ **期望回复及感谢**

- 对于及时的回复(prompt response)深表感谢(grateful)。

求职信

考点回顾

20130323 申请跨国公司的一个职位
20090530 应聘保姆一职

interview ['intəvju:] *n.* 面试，面谈；*vt.* 面试

拓 interviewer *n.* 面谈者，进行面试者
interviewee *n.* 被接见者，被访问者

用 go for an interview 进行面试
to be interviewed for the vacancy
争取空缺职位进行面试
be available for an interview 可以参加面试
grant sb. an interview 给……面试的机会

例 I hope you would consider my application favorably and grant me an interview. 我希望您能认真考虑我的申请，给我面试的机会。

apply [ə'plai] *vi.* 申请，请求

拓 application *n.* 应用，申请；applicant *n.* 申请人

用 apply for 申请；apply for a job 求职

例 I write this letter to apply for the position that you have advertised in newspaper.
我想申请报纸招聘广告上的职位。

inquire about 询问，查问，打听

同 ask for the information 询问信息

例 I am writing to inquire about the entrance to your university.
我想问问关于大学入学的事情。

confidence ['kɔnfidəns] *n.* 信心，信任

反 diffidence *n.* 缺乏自信

用 give one's confidence to… 信任，信赖

have confidence 有信心

例 I have every confidence in my promotion.

我对自己能被升职充满信心。

command [kə'mɑːnd] *n.* 运用能力，掌握，精通

用 at command 掌握，可自由使用

例 I have a good command of international trade and commercial English.

我熟悉国际贸易流程，并熟练掌握商务英语。

creative [kri'eitiv] *adj.* 创造性的

拓 creation *n.* 创造，创作

creativity *n.* 创造力

同 ingenious *adj.* 有独创性的

inventive *adj.* 别出心裁的

用 creative thinking 创造性思维

例 This job is useful and creative.

这项工作既有用又富有创造性。

experience [iks'piəriəns] *n.* 经验，体验

拓 experienced *adj.* 富有经验的

用 working experience 工作经验

practical experience 实践经验

例 As for my working experience, I have been in the administrating position for two years.

至于工作经验，我在行政管理岗位工作了两年。

qualification [ˌkwɔlifi'keiʃən] *n.* 资格，条件

拓 qualify *vt.* 使具有资格；qualified *adj.* 有资格的

同 competence *n.* 能力，胜任

用 qualification and experience 资历
qualification certificate 资格证书
Engineer Qualification Certificate 工程师资格证
Accountant Qualification Certificate 会计师资格证
Computer Operation Qualification Certificate
计算机操作证
Tourist Guide Qualification Certificate 导游证

例 I have a certificate of tourist qualification.
我有导游资格证。

resume ['rezju:mei] *n.* 履历，个人简历

同 curriculum vitae 简历

例 Enclosed with this letter is my resume, which gives further details of my work experience.
随信附上我的简历，里面有我详细的工作经历。

expertise [ˌekspə'ti:z] *n.* 专门知识或技能

用 management expertise 管理技能

例 With our experience, business contacts and expertise, we can overcome problems and arrange everything for you both quickly and efficiently.
以我们的经验、业务联系和专业知识，我们能够克服困难，为您迅速有效地安排好一切。

familiar [fə'miljə] *adj.* 熟悉的

拓 familiarise *vt.* 使熟悉；familiarity *n.* 熟悉，精通

用 be familiar to 为……所熟悉

例 I apply for the tour guide for I am familiar with the place and its people.
我申请导游的职位，因为我熟悉地理民情。

independent [ˌindi'pendənt] *adj.* 独立的，有主见的，有独立见解的，自立的

拓 independence *n.* 独立性；independently *adv.* 独立地

同 self-reliant *adj.* 自力更生的

用 independent thinking 独立思考

例 We should be encouraged to be independent thinkers.
我们应该鼓励独立思考。

consideration [kənˌsidəˈriʃən] *n.* 认为，考虑

拓 reconsider *vt.&vi.* 重新考虑
considerate *adj.* 体谅的，考虑周到的

用 take sth. into consideration 考虑某事

例 Thank you for your consideration and I will be looking forward to your reply.
谢谢您的考虑，期盼您的回复。

链接机经关键词

⊙ 职业申请

- 申请人(applicant)在申请(apply for)一个职位(job vacancy)的时候，首先可以简单介绍一下自己(self-introduction)，从何处得知的招聘信息，如广告上(advertisement)
- 接着介绍自己的教育背景(educational background)，有什么样的毕业证(diploma)和资格(qualification)、证书(certificate)、工作经验(working experience)，你为什么认为自己能胜任这份工作(be qualified for the position，have a good command of English and computer)是必不可少的(it is a must)，当然也包括你的个性 (character/personality)及人际关系的技巧(interpersonal skills)和沟通的技巧(communicational skills)、团队合作精神(team spirit)、竞争意识(sense of competition)、独立精神 (sense of independence)、创造性思维(creative

thinking)等等。

- 基于以上的介绍，相信自己是这一职位的合适人选(I am fully convinced that I am the right person, a good candidate for the job)。
- 说明什么时间可以参加面试(be available for an interview)
- 期望回复(look forward to the opportunity)
- 表示感谢(express thanks)

申请信

考点回顾

20090711 申请住宿
20090321 申请兼职工作

pursue [pə'sju:] *vt.* 寻求，追求；继续

拓 pursuit *n.* 追求

同 seek *vt.&vi.* 寻找

例 I wish to pursue my further education in your university. 我希望有机会在贵校继续深造。

enjoy fame 享有声望

同 well-known *adj.* 著名的，众所周知的
prestigious *adj.* 有名望的，享有声望的

用 enjoy worldwide fame 举世闻名
enjoy fame across the world 举世闻名

例 I choose this university for it enjoys fame across the world. 我选择贵校是因为它享誉海内外。

the possibility of... ……的可能性

用 explore the possibility of sth. 探索……的可能性

例 I am writing to inquire about the possibility of being accepted as a graduate student in your university.
我写信是想询问是否有成为贵校研究生的机会。

admission [əd'miʃən] *n.* 入学；许可；入会费

同 entrance *n.* 入学，进入

用 apply for the admission 申请加入
admission to… 加入

例 I am deeply interested in your graduate programme in your university and plan to apply for admission.
我对贵校的研究生课程很感兴趣，想申请入学。

scholarship ['skɔləʃip] *n.* 学问，学识，学术；奖学金

例 Scholarship scheme is based largely on the examination results at the pre-university level.
奖学金制度很大程度上以入学前的考试成绩为基础。

cherished ['tʃeriʃt] *adj.* 珍贵的，宝贵的

同 treasured *adj.* 珍贵的
precious *adj.* 宝贵的，珍贵的

用 long-cherished wish (desire) 长久的愿望

例 It is my long-cherished desire to pursue study of Computer Science at a university in England.
我一直渴望能在英国大学学习计算机专业。

fulfill [ful'fil]□ *vt.* 履行，满足，实现

拓 fulfillment *n.* 实行，履行

同 achieve *vt.* 完成
accomplish *vt.* 完成

例 I am very excited to set foot on the lovely land to fulfill my years of expectations and long-cherished wish.
能踏上那片可爱的土地，实现我多年的期盼和长久的向往，我感到非常激动。

relevant ['reləvənt] *adj.* 相关的

拓 relevance *n.* 关联

同 related *adj.* 有关联的

例 I would greatly appreciate it if you would send the materials and relevant information at your earliest convenience. 如果您能尽早地给我一些材料和相关的信息，我将非常感谢。

additional [ə'diʃənl] *adj.* 附加的，额外的

同 further *adj.* 另外的，更多的

例 If you need any additional information, please do not hesitate to contact me.
如果您再需要什么信息，请随时和我联系。

tuition [tju'iʃən] *n.* 学费；讲授

同 schooling *n.* 学校教育，学费

用 tuition fee 学费

例 Despite the high tuition fees, a lot of students come to study at Duke University. 尽管杜克大学学费很高，但很多学生仍选择这所学校。

well-equipped [wel, i'kwipt] *adj.* 设备精良的

例 The stadium is well-equipped.
这个运动场设备很好。

well-staffed [wel,stɑ:ft] *adj.* 师资强大的

例 Your university is a well-staffed and well-equipped university with a long history.
贵校的历史悠久，师资强大，设备精良。

procedure [prə'si:dʒə] *n.* 程序；手续

例 Would you please let me know the procedures for admission at your earliest convenience.
请及时通知我关于办理入学手续的相关事宜。

链接机经关键词

- 申请的事情(events)
  - 若是学习(Study Pursuit)，先介绍自己很想参加(attend)某项课程(course)或培训(training programme)，或者很想在该大学继续深造(pursue further study) 或是研究生课程(graduate programme)，询问是否有可能申请入学的机会(inquire about the possibility of admission)。
  - 若是参加体育俱乐部(participate and become the member of the club)，可以表明你选择这所学校的原因(如：Your university is a well-staffed and well-equipped institute with a long history and a fine tradition of scholarship, enjoying a worldwide fame. I will certainly feel greatly honored if I am fortunate enough to be admitted into it.)
- 你的学习计划
  - study plan and arrangement
- 寻求相关的信息
  - additional information like tuition fee, scholarship and admission procedures

推荐信

考点回顾

20010224　向异国同龄人推荐自己的朋友
20050409　为某人推荐入学

candidate ['kændidət] *n.* 候选人，应试者

拓 applicant *n.* 申请人

nominee *n.* 被任命者，被提名的人

例 He is a probable candidate.

他是个有希望的候选人。

ingenious [in'dʒiːnjəs] *adj.* 机灵的，机智的，有独创性的

同 original *adj.* 新颖的，独创的

inspired *adj.* 有灵感的，有创造力的

例 He is an ingenious person who sets out to find the solution to a problem.

他是那种决心去寻求答案且富有创造力的人。

insightful ['inˌsaitful] *adj.* 富于洞察力的，有见识的，有眼光的

用 insightful observation 具有洞察力的观察

例 He gave an extremely profound and insightful response.

他的回答十分深刻而又有见地。

intelligent [in'telidʒənt] *adj.* 聪明的，智能的，理解力强的

拓 intelligence *n.* 智力，理解力

例 Not all intelligent people are good students.

不是每个聪明的人都是好学生。

diligent ['dilidʒənt] *adj.* 勤勉的，用功的

拓 diligence *n.* 勤奋，勤勉

同 industrious *adj.* 勤勉的

hard-working *adj.* 刻苦的

assiduous *adj.* 刻苦的，勤勉的

例 He made a diligent attempt to learn English.

他很勤奋地学习英语。

dedicated ['dedikeitid] *adj.* 专注的，献身的

拓 dedication *n.* 奉献，献身

用 dedicated oneself to... 专心致力于……

例 His whole life is dedicated to scientific research.
他毕生致力于科学研究。

trustworthy ['trʌstˌwəːði] *adj.* 可信赖的，可靠的

同 reliable *adj.* 可靠的，可信赖的
dependable *adj.* 可靠的，可信赖的

例 It is generally admitted that he is a trustworthy person.
大家公认他是个可信赖的人。

perform [pə'fɔːm] *vi.&vt.* 运行；表现

拓 performance *n.* 表演，表现

例 Our team performed very well in the yesterday's games. 在昨天的运动会上我们队表现出色。

链接机经关键词

说明写信的意图

- I am writing to recommend…
- I would like to present …
- With reference to your requirements, I would like to recommend …as an ideal candidate (the right person).

说明推荐的理由

- insightful（富有洞察力）
  intelligent（聪明的）
  dedicated（专注的）
  diligent（勤奋的）
  trustworthy（可信赖的）
- relevant working experience
- be qualified for the position
- Therefore, I think…is worthy of your consideration.
- I therefore recommend…without any reservation

邀请信

考点回顾

20130309 邀请朋友看运动比赛
20090926 邀请朋友的父母

invite [in'vait] *vt.* 邀请，招待；*n.* 邀请

拓 invitation *n.* 邀请
inviter *n.* 邀请者

用 invite sb. to dinner 请某人吃饭
invite in 请……入内，邀请……到家里
invite sb. to do... 邀请某人……

例 They invited us to their party, and we reciprocated their invitation. 他们邀请我们参加宴会，我们也回报了他们的邀请。

写作提示

开篇点题：
I am writing to invite you to...
给您写信想要请您……
I wonder if you could come to...
我想知道您是否能参加……

attend [ə'tend] *vt.&vi.* 出席，参加

拓 attendance *n.* 出席，到场

同 participate *vi.* 参与，参加；*vt.* 分享
take part in 参加

用 attend a lecture/meeting/party/school
听讲座/出席会议/参加聚会/上学

例 I am writing to ask whether you would be willing to attend the celebration in our community. 我写信想问您是否愿意参加我们社区举办的庆祝活动。

celebrate ['selibreit] *vt.&vi.* 庆祝

用 celebrate a festival 庆祝节日，过节

例 The Chinese celebrate their New Year in January or February. 中国人在1月或2月庆祝新年。

in advance 预先，提前

同 ahead *adv.* 预先，提前

例 In that case, you should inform them in advance. 如果是那样的话，你必须事前通知他们。

honour ['ɔnə] *n.* 荣誉，头衔

拓 honourary *adj.* 荣誉的，名誉的

honourable *adj.* 光荣的，高贵的

用 uphold the honour of one's country 维护国家的荣誉

例 Her honour was discredited in the newspapers. 她的名声被报纸败坏了。

链接机经关键词

⊙ 邀请参加的活动

- birthday party, celebration，public event in the community

⊙ 地点、时间

- in the neighborhood, home, park, club, school

⊙ 询问是否可以参加

- I wondered if you are available to attend, take part in this activity.

- feel honored if you could come

⊙ 期望回复

- Look forward to a reply.
- Tell us whether you can come or not in advance.

建议信

考点回顾

20100508 给培训组织者的建议
20090613 给老师的建议
20090418 选专业方面的建议

suggest [sə'dʒest] *vt.* 提议，建议

拓 suggestion *n.* 建议

同 propose *vt.&vi.* 建议

advise *vt.&vi.* 建议

用 suggest sb. to do sth. 建议某人做某事

例 I would like to suggest that you choose the business management as your major.

我建议你选择商务管理作为你的专业。

recommend [ˌrekə'mend] *vt.&vi.* 推荐；建议

拓 recommendation *n.* 推荐；推荐信

同 advise *vt.&vi.* 建议

suggest *vt.* 提议，建议

用 recommend sb. sth. 推荐某人做某事

例 What restaurant in this city do you recommend?

你会推荐这座城市的哪家餐馆?

put forward 提出，拿出

用 put forward a suggestion(proposal/plan) 提出建议

例 Mary put forward a constructive suggestion at the meeting. 玛丽在会上提出了一个建设性的建议。

advise [əd'vaiz] *vt.&vi.* 建议

拓 advice *n.* 建议

例 It is easy for you to advise, but difficult to take advice from others.
劝告别人容易，接受劝告就难了。

feasible ['fi:zəbl] *adj.* 可行的，可实行的

拓 feasibility *n.* 可行性，可能性

同 attainable *adj.* 可达到的
workable *adj.* 切实可行的
practical *adj.* 实际的，实用性的

反 infeasible *adj.* 不可实行的
unpractical *adj.* 不切实际的

用 a feasible plan/suggestion 可实施的方案/建议

例 Compared with the other method, the method is efficient and feasible.
通过与其他方法比较，这个方法是有效可行的。

practical ['præktikəl] *adj.* 实际的，实用性的

同 applicable *adj.* 可应用的
feasible *adj.* 可行的，可实行的
practicable *adj.* 可实行的

用 for (all) practical purposes 实际上
practical experience 实际经验

例 Please contact me if you think the suggestion is practical and need further information about improving the service in the library.
如果您认为我的建议有实用价值且需要关于提升图书馆服务质量的进一步信息，请与我联系。

take...into account 考虑

同 take...into consideration 考虑

例 I would be grateful indeed if you can take my suggestion into account.
如果您能认真考虑我的建议，我将非常感谢。

in reply to 答复，回应

同 in response to 回应

例 I am writing in reply to your advertisement for a salesperson. 我写信是想应聘你们招聘广告上销售人员的职位。

链接机经关键词

写信目的——提出建议

- I would like to offer my suggestions about upgrading its equipment in the library in the neighborhood.

建议类型

- 给朋友提出建议，如国外留学选课(select course)以及食宿(accommodation)等；
- 给活动的组织者(organiser)提出建议，如培训课程(a training course)的反馈(feedback)等；
- 给图书馆提出建议，如图书馆(library)设备更新(equipment upgrading)等。

你为什么提出这样的建议

- Why do you think it is feasible or practical?
- 期望收信者能够考虑该建议(take my suggestion into account)。

Unit 2

Writing Task 2 高频词汇

本单元主要讲雅思大作文的主题词汇，分为：

- 教育题材
- 科技题材
- 环境题材
- 工作题材
- 媒体题材
- 国际化与发展题材
- 社会与生活题材
- 政府政策题材
- 犯罪题材
- 动物题材

根据最新真题，提炼高频词汇；同时在链接机经关键词中，选取典型代表题目，给出写作思路，并将词汇及短语一一标出，既有助于拓展思路，又能帮助考生了解高频词汇。

1. 教育题材

考点回顾

教育方式

20120901 学生在校表现不好则被禁止上学
20100715 自学技能还是通过向老师学习
20100515 远程教育与大学教育
20090425 网络教育与课堂教育

课程选择

A类题目
20130223 选择与科学相关课程的大学生变少了
20100520 孩子应该遵守规则，还是应该宽松管理
20100508 专业课和音乐、体育课，哪个对未来的职业有用
20090926 高中毕业是应该先工作还是先旅行
20090813 课程由政府决定还是由老师决定
20090620 学习外语的重要性
20090509 是学习所有的课程还是只学习感兴趣的课程
G类题目
20091212 传统课程与沟通技巧，商务课，哪个更重要
20091107 学生在业余时间是否应该学习

教育目的

20091024 大学教育的功能

education [ˌedjuːˈkeiʃən] *n.* 教育；教育学；培养

拓 educate *vt.* 教育；educated *adj.* 受过教育的

educational *adj.* 教育的

用 receive education 接受教育

student-oriented education 以学生为主体的教育

quality-oriented education 素质教育

distance education 远程教育

on-line education 网络教育

vocational education 职业教育

primary-level education 小学教育

secondary-level education 中学教育

tertiary-level education 大学教育

例 Education systems are based on the belief that all children can effectively be taught to acquire different skills. 教育体制的理念在于能够教会所有孩子掌握各种技能。

schooling [ˈskuːliŋ] *n.* 学校教育

同 education *n.* 教育；tuition *n.* 学费；讲授

例 Rather than breaking up family by sending children to the school, education authorities have been able to use the Internet to deliver schooling online.

教育当局已经能实现网络教学，所以不用将孩子送到学校而与家人分离。

背景拓展

现在中国实行的是义务教育(compulsory schooling)，目标是为了实现普及教育(universal schooling)。一般在义务教育阶段采取全日制教育(full-time schooling)，义务教育阶段包括小学教育(elementary schooling)和中学教育(secondary schooling)。

schooling除了有“教育”的意思，还有“学费，学校膳宿费”的意思。

parenting ['peərəntiŋ] *n.* 父母对子女的养育

同 home-schooling *n.* 在家教育

例 Perhaps parenting classes are needed to help them to do this, and high quality nursery schools could be established and would support families more in terms of raising next generation. 也许需要设立家长课堂来辅助他们培养孩子。就抚养下一代而言，也应该开办高质量的幼儿园来辅助家长。

home schooling 在家教育，家庭学校

例 Home schooling in modern sense is an alternative in developed countries to formal education. 在发达国家具有时代特征的家教育方式可以替代学校教育方式。

写作提示

家庭学校(home schooling)指儿童在家接受教育，主要由父母承担教学任务，扮演学校中教师的角色。这一解释是相对于学校教育而言的。

distance-learning [distəns'lə:niŋ] *n.* 远程学习

同 on-line learning 网络学习

例 Living in such an information-explosion era, people can acquire knowledge from different approaches, such as watching TV, surfing the Internet, listening to lectures as well as the distance-learning. 生活在信息爆炸的时代，人们可以通过各种途径来获取知识，如，看电视、上网、听讲座以及远程教育。

primary school 小学

例 In many places today, children start primary school at around the age of six or seven. 如今很多地方，孩子在六七岁的时候就上小学了。

replace [ri'pleis] *vt.* 取代，代替

拓 replacement *n.* 更换；replaceable *adj.* 可替换的

irreplaceable *adj.*不能替代的

同 substitute *vi.&vt.* 代替；take the place of 代替

用 replaced with… 用……代替

例 If the schooling is replaced by the on-line learning, then the lack of personal interaction would become the major concern. 如果学校教育被网络教育取代，那么最主要的问题将是师生间缺乏沟通。

complement ['kɔmplimənt] *n.* 补充，补足

拓 complementary *adj.* 补充的

同 supplement *n.* 补充

用 A is a complement to B. = A is a supplement to B. A是B的补充。

例 Distance learning has greatly benefited many people. But it is still a complement to normal education. 远程教育给人们带来很多的好处，但仍然是正规教育的补充。

instill [in'stil] *vt.* 逐渐灌输

拓 instillation *n.* 慢慢灌输；instillment *n.* 慢慢灌输

同 impart *vt.* 给予（尤指抽象事物），传授
inculcate *vt.* 谆谆教诲，反复灌输

用 instill high moral values 灌输高尚的道德观
instill an idea into sb.'s mind
把思想灌输到某人头脑中

例 It is easy to instill the minds of young children with fixed ideas. 很容易将固定的观念灌输给孩子们。

impart [im'pɑ:t] *vt.* 给予，传授

拓 impartation *n.* 给予；imparted *adj.* 给予的

用 impart knowledge to… 传授知识给……

例 The good teacher imparts wisdom to his pupils.
好的老师把智慧传授给学生。

inculcation [in'kʌlkeiʃən] *n.* 谆谆教诲，教授

拓 inculcate *vt.* 教育

用 inculcate an idea upon sb. 向某人反复灌输某一思想

inculcate the young with a sense of duty
向年轻人灌输责任感

例 The responsibilities of a teacher lie not only in the inculcation of knowledge, but also in the setting of good examples and cultivation of virtues. 老师的责任不但是传授知识，更重要的是树立良好榜样，培养学生的品德。

cultivate ['kʌltiveit] *vt.* 培养，耕作，陶冶

拓 cultivated *adj.* 有教养的；cultivation *n.* 培养

同 foster *vt.* 培养；nurture *vt.* 养育；develop *vt.* 开发

用 cultivate the sense of... 培养……意识

例 It takes some time to cultivate a new friendship.
建立一段新的友谊需要一段时间。

enhance [in'hɑ:ns] *vt.* 提高；增加，加强

拓 enhancement *n.* 增加；enhanced *adj.* 增大的；加强的

同 better *vt.* 改善；improve *vt.* 改善
uplift *vt.* 提高；boost *vt.* 促进

用 enhance one's competitiveness in the future job-seeking 提高未来的职场竞争力

enhance one's teamwork spirit and competitive consciousness 提高团队精神和竞争意识

例 The computer can enhance the quality of photographs transmitted from space.
计算机可增强从太空发回的照片的清晰度。

motivate ['məutiveit] *vt.* 刺激，使有动机，激发……的积极性

拓 motivation *n.* 动机，积极性
motivated *adj.* 有动机的，有积极性的

同 inspire *vt.* 激发，鼓舞

用 motivate the students to do sth. 鼓励学生去做某事

例 A good teacher has to be able to motivate her students. 好教师必须激发学生积极学习。

stimulate ['stimjuleit] *vt.* 刺激，鼓舞，激励

拓 stimulating *adj.* 刺激的；stimulation *n.* 激励，鼓舞；stimulative *adj.* 促进的，激励的

同 spur *vt.* 激励，鞭策；invigorate *vt.* 鼓舞
energize *vt.* 激励

用 stimulate one's interest 激发了某人的兴趣
stimulate economic development 刺激经济发展
stimulate domestic demand 刺激国内需求

例 In conclusion, I would say that change can be stimulating and energizing for individuals when they pursue it themselves, but that all change, including that which is imposed on people, does not necessarily have good outcomes. 总之，我认为当人们追求改变的时候，某种改变会鼓励他们或使他们变得有活力。但并不是人们身上发生的所有改变，都会产生好的结果。

secure [si'kjuə] *vt.* 得到，获得；确立，促成

用 secure a decent job 得到体面的工作
secure information 得到信息
secure one's reputation 确立了某人的好名声

例 Today, education has become a priority for many parents seeking to secure a good future for their children in this rapidly changing world. 在现在日益变化的世界里，家长为给孩子谋求一个好的未来，首先考虑的是教育问题。

break [breik] *n.* 休息；中断

例 It is quite common these days for young people in many countries to have a break from studying after graduating from high school. 最近很多国家的年轻人在高中毕业后过间隔年，再继续学业。这是普遍的现象。

背景知识

间隔年是西方国家的青年在升学或者毕业之后、工作之前，做一次长期的旅行（通常是一年），让学生在步入社会之前体验社会生活。在间隔年期间，学生在旅行的同时通常也适当做一些与自己专业相关的工作或者一些非政府组织的志愿者工作，他们相信，这样更加有利于学生找到更好的工作或者找到自己真正想要的工作，从而更好地融入社会。

feedback ['fi:dbæk] *n.* 反馈，反馈信息

同 response *n.* 反应；reaction *n.* 反应

用 students' feedback 学生的反馈

例 Firstly, a person needs to feel that he is doing valuable work, so positive feedback from superiors is very important in this respect. 首先，一个人应感到他所从事的是有价值的工作，因而从上司那里得到积极的反馈是很重要的。

appraise [ə'preiz] *vt.* 评价，鉴定，估价

拓 appraisement *n.* 评价； appraisal *n.* 评价

同 assess *vt.* 评定；appreciate *vt.* 鉴别
evaluate *vt.* 评价

用 students appraise/evaluate their teacher's performance 学生评价老师的教学

例 A dealer came to appraise the furniture.
一个商人对家具进行了估价。

adapt [ə'dæpt] *vt.* 使适应；*vi.* 适应

拓 adaptability *n.* 适应性；adaptable *adj.* 能适应的

同 adjust *vt.* 调整；accustom *vt.* 使习惯于

用 adapt oneself to sth. 使自己适应某事

adapt oneself to the development of...
使自己适应……的发展

例 Young adults may end up with never returning to their studies or finding it difficult to adapt to the academic environment again. 结果可能是年轻人不会继续学业，或者很难重新适应学习环境。

perspective [pə'spektiv] *n.* 观点

同 outlook *n.* 观点；viewpoint *n.* 观点，视角
standpoint *n.* 立场，观点

用 in one's perspective 就某人的观点而言

例 That is the best way for them to get a clear perspective of what they are hoping to do with their lives and why. 这是他们明确自己生活目标及为什么是这个目标的最好途径。

achieve [ə'tʃiːv] *vt.* 完成，达到；*vi.* 达到目的

同 complete *vt.* 完成；fulfill *vt.* 实现
accomplish *vt.* 实现

例 Overall, I think an ability to keep clear perspectives in life is a more essential factor in achieving happiness. 总之，我认为明确自己的人生目标是获得幸福的重要因素。

acquire [ə'kwaiə] *vt.* 获得，学到，取得

拓 acquisitive *adj.* 获得的；acquisition *n.* 获得

同 gain *vt.* 获得；obtain *vt.* 获得；secure *vt.* 获得

例 Their brains are still programmed to acquire their mother tongue, which facilitates learning another language. 他们的大脑组织还是处于学习母语的阶段，这其实有利于学习另一语言。

excel [ik'sel] *vt.&vi.* 优于，擅长

拓 excellence *n.* 优秀，长处

同 exceed *vt.&vi* 超过，胜过；surpass *vt.* 超越，胜过

例 Such talents can give individuals a facility for certain skills that allow them to excel, while more hard-working students never manage to reach a comparable level. 这些具有天赋的人能够在某些方面出类拔萃，这可能是那些勤奋的人也无法企及的。

academic [ˌækə'demik] *adj.* 学院的，学术的，理论的

拓 academically *adv.* 学术上

用 academic activities 学术活动

academic atmosphere 学习氛围

academic performance 学习成绩

academic exchange 学术交流

例 If everything they do must have some educational or academic relevance, then they will soon get tired of studying altogether, which is the last thing parents would want. 如果他们所做的任何一件事必须与教育或学术相关，那么他们将很快就厌恶学习，这是父母最不愿意看到的事情。

talent ['tælənt] *n.* 才能，天资，天才

拓 talented *adj.* 有才能的；talentless *adj.* 无能的

同 capacity *n.* 能力；endowment *n.*天资；aptitude *n.*天资

用 nurture a student's talent 培养学生的才能

explore one's talent 发挥个人才干

例 Without the natural talent, continuous training would be neither attractive nor productive, and without the training, the child would not learn how to exploit their talent. 没有天赋，即使是持续不断的训练也是既无吸引力又无进展的，而要是没有刻苦的训练，孩子也不会学会如何发挥自己的能力。

knowledge ['nɔlidʒ] *n.* 知识，学问

拓 knowledgeable *adj.* 知识渊博的

用 pursue knowledge 追求知识

thirst for knowledge 渴求知识

enlarge a scope of knowledge 扩大知识面

例 However, if there are different kinds of happiness for different individuals then the first step in achieving it would be to have a degree of self-knowledge. 然而，如果说不同的人对幸福的理解不同，那么获得幸福的第一步是在一定程度上了解自己。

well-bred [wel͵bred] *adj.* 教养良好的，有教养的

同 well-cultivated *adj.* 有教养的

反 ill-bred *adj.* 没教养的

例 None but the well-bred man knows how to confess a fault, or acknowledge himself in an error.
唯有有教养的人才知道如何承认错误，或意识到自己的行为是错误的 。

enterprising spirit 进取心，进取精神，创业精神

同 pioneering spirit 开拓精神

例 All great wisdom in life are contained in these words by Gump's mother: optimism, strong mind and enterprising spirit, calmness and bluntness, religious and faithful belief.
这些话语中包含了阿甘的母亲面对生活的种种大智慧：积极乐观的心态，刚毅进取的精神，坦然率直的态度，虔诚忠实的信仰。

distinguish [dis'tiŋgwiʃ] *vt.&vi.* 辨别，区分

拓 distinguishable *adj.*可辨识的

distinguished *adj.* 著名的

用 distinguish right from wrong 明辨是非

distinguish one thing from another
将一事物与另一事物区别开来

例 Children should be taught to distinguish right from wrong, which is the responsibility of both the parents and teachers. 应该教会孩子们明辨是非，这既是家长又是教师的责任。

mental development 心智发展，心理发展过程

拓 mentality *n.* 智能，智心

例 Today the way we consider human psychology and mental development is heavily influenced by the genetic sciences. 当今，我们认为人们的心理和心智发育很大程度上受基因的影响。

raise [reiz] *vt.* 养育

同 bring up 教育，养育

用 raise the children to be... 将孩子抚养成……

例 If they could raise the children to be considerate of others and to be social, responsible individuals, the whole community would benefit. 如果他们将孩子培养成为关心他人、善于交际、有责任感的人，那么整个社会也将受益。

discipline ['disiplin] *n.* 纪律；学科

拓 disciplined *adj.* 遵守纪律的
well-disciplined *adj.* 训练有素的
undisciplined *adj.*无纪律的

例 When they get to school age they have not learnt any self-control or discipline. 他们到了上学的年龄，仍然没有自控能力或纪律性。

sense [sens] *n.* 意识，认识

同 awareness *n.* 意识；recognition *n.* 识别

用 sense of obligation (responsibility) 责任感

sense of fulfillment 成就感
sense of belonging to a team 团队归属感
sense of achievement 成就感

例 Satisfaction is also increased by a sense of responsibility for and loyalty to a team.
责任意识和对团队的忠诚度也能增强满足感。

characteristic [ˌkæriktəˈristik] *n.* 特性，特征

同 personality traits 个性品质

例 But whether these characteristics are able to develop within the personality of an individual surely depends on whether the circumstances allow such a development. 但是个性是否能够得到发展，这肯定要取决于外部的环境因素。

shape one's personality 塑造个性

例 It is the interaction of the two that shapes a person's personality and dictates how that personality develops.
两者的相互作用能塑造一个人的个性，并决定个性的发展。

moral [ˈmɔːrəl] *adj.* 道德的，精神上的，品行端正的；*n.* 道德

用 moral guidance 道德指引； moral standard 道德水准
moral value 道德观； moral appeals 伦理
moral behavior 道德行为； moral education 道德教育
morals and ethics 思想道德修养

例 Universities exist for the purposes such as improving students' well-round development and raising students' moral standards. 大学教育的作用是促进学生的全面发展，并提高学生的道德水准。

intellectual [ˌintiˈlektjuəl] *adj.* 智力的，聪明的，理智的

用 intellectual development 智力发展
intellectual faculties 智能

intellectual activities 智力活动

intellectual and ideological development
精神文明建设

intellectual education 智育

例 It is important to remember that children need to develop skills other than intellectual ones, and the best way to do this through activities such as sports, games and playing with other kids. 很重要的一点是孩子们不仅需要发展智力，而且需要培养各种技能，而最好的方法就是通过体育、游戏这样的活动和其他的孩子们一起玩耍。

intelligence [in'telidʒəns] *n.* 智力，理解力

拓 intelligent *adj.* 智能的

例 One thing that puts man above animals is intelligence. 促使人类凌驾于动物之上的一点就是人类有智慧。

potential [pə'tenʃəl] *n.* 可能性；潜能

拓 potentiality *n.* 潜力； potentialize *vt.*使具有潜力

同 possibility *n.* 可能性

用 tap the potential 挖掘……的潜力

fulfill one's potential 发挥潜力

draw out a child's potential capacities 开发孩子的潜能

例 It is important to draw out a child's potential capacities. 开发孩子的潜力是很重要的。

innate [i'neit] *adj.* 先天的，固有的，与生俱来的

同 inborn *adj.* 天生的

用 have an innate talent for sth. 某方面有天赋

例 Young children's innate abilities should be harnessed to make these benefits more achievable. 小孩儿天生的能力应得到管束，以使其优势发挥得更加淋漓尽致。

nature ['neitʃə] *n.* 自然，本性

拓 natural *adj.* 自然的，天生的

用 against (contrary to) nature 违反自然的，反常的

back to nature 回归大自然；by nature 生性，本性上

by the light of nature 本能地，自然而然地

in nature 实际上；second nature 第二天性

in someone's nature 在某人的禀性之中

例 It is human nature to hate repetition work.

讨厌重复工作是人的天性。

nurture ['nə:tʃə] *vt.* 养育；鼓励

拓 nurturance *n.* 养成，教育

同 raise *vt.*养育； foster *vt.* 培养，养育；nourish *vt.* 抚养

用 nurture imagination 培养想象力

例 But, as with all questions of nature versus nurture, they are not mutually exclusive. 考虑到天赋与后天培育，二者并不相互排斥。

strive for 争取，奋斗

同 struggle *vi.* 奋斗； spare no effort 不遗余力

用 strive for excellence 追求卓越

例 We must have clear goals and great dreams in our life and strive for it with whole life!我们的人生必须有明确的目标和伟大的理想并且要为之奋斗一生！

be endowed with 被赋予，天生具有

同 be born with 天生具有

例 Therefore, every child should be endowed with the right to handle their own problems within their abilities. 因此，每个孩子都应该被赋予在能力所及范围内处理自己的问题的自由。

versatile ['və:sətail] *adj.* 多才多艺的，万能的，多面手的

拓 versatility *n.* 多才多艺

generalist 通才；specialist 专才
physical and mental development 身心全面发展
psychological soundness 心理健康
psychological well-being (welfare) 心理健康
all-round development 全面发展

同 many-sided *adj.* 多方面的
all-around *adj.* 全面的
well-rounded *adj.* 多才多艺的

例 A versatile person is often good at a number of different things. 多才多艺的人通常擅长许多种不同的事情。

competence ['kɔmpitəns] *n.* 能力，胜任

拓 competent *adj.* 胜任的
incompetent *adj.* 无能力的，不胜任的

用 core competence 核心竞争力

例 Cultural strength is the source of core competence in enterprise. 文化力是企业核心竞争力的源泉。

misguide [mis'gaid] *vt.* 误导，使误入歧途

拓 guide *vt.* 引导； misguiding *adj.* 误导的

同 mislead *vt.* 误导

用 be misguided by… 被……误导了

例 However, the parents who do not allow their children sufficient free time for leisure activities outside school hours, are misguided. 然而，那些剥夺孩子们课余时间的家长被误导了。

aptitude ['æptitju:d] *n.* 能力，才能，才智，天资

同 talent *n.* 才能；ability *n.* 能力； skill *n.* 技能

用 have an aptitude for 有……的才能
show an aptitude for 显示出……才能

例 Even as a child he showed an unusual aptitude for mathematics. 甚至孩童时他就显露出非同一般的数学才能。

horizon [həˈraizən] *n.* 眼界，范围，视野

同 perspective *n.* 观点

用 enlarge/broaden one's horizon 开阔视野

例 My view is that young people should be encouraged to broaden their horizons.

我的观点是应该鼓励年轻人去开阔视野。

independent [ˌindiˈpendənt] *adj.* 独立的

拓 independence *n.* 独立性；independently *adv.* 独立地

dependent *adj.* 依靠的

例 They are generally more confident and independent than children who stay at home with their parents and who are not used to strangers or new situations.

相对那些待在家里的孩子们以及那些不适应与陌生人打交道或不适应新环境的人来说，他们往往更加自信、独立。

economically independent 经济独立

同 financially independent 经济独立

例 It is also evident among poorer students who choose to work and become economically independent for a period of time. 很明显，穷人家的孩子为了经济上的独立会选择出去工作一段时间。

socially [ˈsəuʃəli] *adv.* 在社会上，善于交际地，在社交方面

拓 social *adj.* 社会的；sociable *adj.* 社交的

unsociable *adj.* 不爱交际的

例 Another advantage of going to school at an early age is that children can develop faster socially.

早上学的另外一个好处是孩子们能很快地培养与人交际的能力。

expertise [ˌekspəˈtiːz] *n.* 专门知识或技能

同 knowledge *n.* 知识；skill *n.* 技能

例 We were amazed at his expertise on the ski slopes.
他在斜坡滑雪方面的技能令我们赞叹不已。

extra-curricular [ˌekstrəkə'rikjulə] *adj.* 课外的

用 extra-curricular activities 课外活动

例 A variety of extra-curricular activities are arranged for all students.
学校为学生安排了多种课外活动。

scope [skəup] *n.* 视野，眼界；范围

同 range *n.* 范围；sphere *n.* 范围；extent *n.* 范围

用 scope of knowledge 知识面

例 In a sense, watching TV can enlarge the scope of knowledge with vivid pictures. 一定意义上来说，看电视可以通过生动的画面来扩大知识面。

overseas study 海外学习

同 go abroad for further study 出国留学

例 Disorientation, loneliness, homesickness and depression are all the problems students abroad encounter in their overseas study. 无方向感、孤独、思乡和压抑是留学生在海外学习中会遇到的障碍。

背景拓展

Advantages of overseas study:

ambition and desire to learn 雄心和学习的热望
cultivate the ability of self-learning 培养自学能力
expand one's knowledge 扩展知识
build up the friendship 建立友谊
spirit of cooperation and competition 合作与竞争精神
broaden one's horizon 开阔眼界
team spirit 团队精神
creation and originality 创造力与独创性
remove loneliness and disorientation
消除孤独感和不适应感
cross-cultural communication 跨文化交际

contribute to 有助于

同 be helpful to 有助于；be beneficial to 有益于

例 Of course, factors such as loving relationships, good health, the skills to earn a living and a peaceful environment all contribute to our happiness. 当然，良好的感情、健康的体魄、谋生的技能以及安定的生活环境等诸如此类的因素，都会使我们感到幸福。

add spice to 增添情趣

同 add flavor to 增添情趣

用 add spice to daily life 增加生活情趣

例 We need a trip to add some spice to our lives.
我们想通过旅游来调剂一下生活。

interpret [in'tə:prit] *vt.* 把……理解为，领会

拓 interpretation *n.* 解释，理解

同 understand *vt.* 理解

用 people interpret…in many different ways
人们对……有不同的理解

例 Because people interpret happiness for themselves in so many different ways, it is difficult to give any definition that is true for everyone.
因为人们定义幸福的方法多种多样，很难给出适合于每一个人的定义。

awareness [ə'weənis] *n.* 意识，认识

拓 aware *adj.* 意识到的；unaware *adj.*没意识到的

同 sense *n.* 感觉；consciousness *n.* 意识

用 enhance (raise) awareness of … 提升……意识

例 Like self-awareness, this is also very difficult to achieve it, but I think these are the two factors that maybe the most important for achieving happiness. 很难能对自我有清楚的认识，但是我认为这两种因素可能对于获得幸福最重要。

attend [ə'tend] *vt.* 出席，上（大学等）

拓 attendance *n.* 出席；attendant *adj.* 伴随的

用 attend a lecture 上课；attend by 伴着

例 So overall, I believe that, attending school from a young age is good for most children. 总之，我认为早上学对大多数的孩子来说是有益的。

environment [in'vairənmənt] *n.* 环境；氛围

同 circumstance *n.* 环境

用 learning environment 学习氛围

例 They still spend plenty of time at home with their parents, so they can benefit from both environments. 他们仍然可以在家里和父母在一起，因此他们从两种环境中都可以受益。

nursery school 幼儿园

例 Instead, they will probably go to a nursery school when they are much younger. 相反，他们可能很小的时候就去上幼儿园。

interact [ˌintə'rækt] *vt.&vi.* 相互作用，相互影响

拓 interactive *adj.*相互作用的；interaction *n.* 相互作用

用 interact with 互动

例 First, a child will learn to interact with a lot of different people and some children learn to communicate very early because of this. 首先，孩子可以学着和不同的人接触，正因为如此，一些孩子在很早的时候就学会了沟通。

learning ['lə:niŋ] *n.* 学习；学问

用 self-learning *n.*自学

independent thinking and learning 独立思考和学习

例 Overseas study can develop the ability of independent thinking and learning. 海外求学能够培养人独立思考和学习的能力。

instruction [in'strʌkʃən] *n.* 教授，指导

拓 instruct *vt.* 教，讲授

instructive *adj.* 有益的，教育性的

例 In class, the teacher creates a friendly and relaxed atmosphere by listening to them and giving them instructions if necessary.

课堂上，老师通过倾听并在必要的时候给予恰当的引导，为学生创造了一种和谐而轻松的氛围。

enlighten [in'laitn] *vt.* 启发，启蒙，教导

拓 enlightened *adj.* 开明的

enlightening *adj.* 有启发作用的

enlightenment *n.* 启蒙

同 illuminate *vt.* 阐明； clarify *vt.* 澄清，阐明

instruct *vt.* 指导

例 Educating means offering thoughts and opening minds, and it should enlighten students on thinking.

教育意味着启迪思想，开发智力，而且应该引导学生去思考。

inspire [in'spaiə] *vt.* 鼓舞，激发，启示，使产生灵感

拓 inspiring *adj.* 鼓舞人心的，启发灵感的

inspiration *n.* 灵感，鼓舞

同 motivate *vt.* 刺激，使有动机

enlighten *vt.* 启发，启蒙

kindle *vt.* 点燃；激起

用 inspire sth. in sb. 使某人产生某种感情

inspire children's creativity 启发孩子的创造力

inspire sb. to do sth. 启发某人做某事

例 Teachers should inspire the students to have the enthusiasm for knowledge, life and friendship.

教师应该激发学生对知识、生活及友情的热爱。

spooned [spu:nd] *adj.* 娇生惯养的，受到保护的，受填鸭式教育的

拓 duck-stuffing teaching 填鸭式教学
cramming education 填鸭式教学

例 Students should cultivate the ability of self-learning rather than being spooned. 学生应该培养自学的能力，而不是强行被灌输知识。

concentrate on 集中精力于

同 focus on 集中注意力于；be immersed in 沉浸于
be dedicated to 致力于；be devoted to 专心于

例 Many young people cannot concentrate on study as a result of being addicted to playing computer games.
很多年轻人由于沉迷于电脑游戏而不能集中精力学习。

preoccupation [pri,ɔkju'peiʃən] *n.* 全神贯注，入神

拓 preoccupied *adj.* 全神贯注的

用 take one's preoccupation with 专心致志

例 Environmental protection is clearly their main preoccupation. 很明显环保是他们的工作重点。

corporal punishment 体罚

同 physical punishment 体罚

例 Corporal punishment inflicts deep psychological wounds on children.
体罚会对孩子造成极深的心理伤害。

foundation [faun'deiʃən] *n.* 基础，地基

用 lay a solid foundation for 为……打下坚实的基础

例 Good academic performance will lay a solid foundation for future career.
良好的学业会为未来的职业打下坚实的基础。

have a keen interest in 对……有强烈的兴趣

拓 stimulate one's interest 激发兴趣

lose interest in 对……失去兴趣

例 Foreign students usually have a keen interest in local culture and food. 留学生通常会对当地的文化及美食有浓厚的兴趣。

get accustomed to 适应，习惯于

同 be accustomed to 习惯于；be adaptable to 适应于

例 Only a better understanding of this nation can help you get accustomed to and integrate with it.

只有更加了解这个国家，才能够习惯它并融入到它的生活中去。

critical thinking 批判性思考

拓 independent thinking 独立思考

例 Emphasis continues to be placed on promoting students' judgment and critical thinking. 学校课程继续着重培养学生的判断力和批判性思考能力。

perception [pə'sepʃən] *n.* 认识，观念

例 It is quite understandable that people from different backgrounds have different perception on the same issue. 不同背景的人们对同一事件的态度各异是非常可以理解的。

链接机经关键词

⊙ 教育

- 学校教育(schooling)与家庭教育(parenting)是孩子成长过程中不可或缺的(indispensable)教育方式，对孩子的身心发育(physical and mental development)起着重要的作用。家庭教育(upbringing)可以给

孩子正确的引导，帮助他们树立正确的世界观(world outlook)、人生观(outlook on life)和价值观(values)。学校教育的优势在于学生生活在集体的氛围中(environment)，可以培养其竞争意识、合作精神和独立性(cultivate sense of competition, sense of cooperation and independence)。理想中的学校应该满足学生全面发展的要求(development in an all-round way)。

- 出国留学和寄宿学校的优势在于能够培养学生的独立能力(independence)、适应能力(adaptability)、应对危机的能力(crisis-solving)、解决问题的能力(problem-solving)、建立友谊(build up friendship)、沟通的能力(communication skills)、建立良好的人际关系的能力(interpersonal relationship)和独立思考的能力(independent thinking)。

2. 科技题材

考点回顾

A类题目

20130323 科技对人类生活的影响

20100320 很多工作被机器取代

20100227 科技发展的利弊

20091212 在家办公，只有员工受益

20090808 科技改变了人与人之间的关系

20090117 交通使人们可以在任何地方工作和生活

20090110 科技是否加大了贫富差距

G类题目
20100417 手机对年轻人的影响
20100109 手机的利弊
20090926 计算机的利弊

breakthrough ['breik,θru:] *n.* 突破，突破性进展

用 technological breakthrough 科技突破

例 Technological and scientific breakthroughs are changing the whole way we view the world.
科学技术的突破日益改变着人们看待世界的方式。

beyond one's expectations 超出想象

例 Over the last half century the pace of change in the life of human beings has increased beyond our expectations. 上半个世纪以来，人类生活的变化之快超出我们的想象。

technological [,teknə'lɔdʒikəl] *adj.* 技术的，工艺的

拓 technology *n.* 技术，工艺

用 technological innovation 科技创新

例 The recent two decades witnessed the boom of science and technology, which gave rise to a series of technological innovations. 近二十年，科技的发展带动了系列科技产品的创新。

advance [əd'vɑ:ns] *vt.&vi.* 发展，促进，提高，提升

拓 advancement *n.* 前进，进步； advanced *adj.* 先进的

同 accelerate *vt.&vi.* 加速，促进
promote *vt.* 促进，提升

例 We had greatly advanced in our knowledge of the world. 我们在世界知识方面大有长进。

forge ahead 稳步前进

例 Our work has been forging ahead recently.
近来，我们的工作一直在稳步进行。

by leaps and bounds 飞跃地，突飞猛进地

例 Science and technology advances by leaps and bounds. 科技发展日新月异。

sweep away 清除，扫除

同 clear away 清除

例 The Internet, fax machines, satellites, and cable TV are sweeping away cultural boundaries and changing the perceptions of the general public. 互联网、传真、卫星和有线电视扫清了国家间的文化障碍，改变了大众观念。

interdependent [ˌintədiˈpendənt] *adj.* 互相依赖的，互相依存的

拓 interdependence *n.* 互相依赖

例 Airplanes, telephone service, email and computers have made the world more interdependent than ever. 飞机、电话、邮件及电脑使世界变得比以往更加相互依赖。

efficiency [iˈfiʃənsi] *n.* 效率，功效，效能

拓 efficient *adj.* 有效率的

反 inefficiency *n.* 无效率

用 achieve the high efficiency 获得高效
enhance the efficiency 提高效率

例 The obvious benefit of air travel is that it can enhance the efficiency and facilitate cultural and economic interaction between countries.
乘飞机旅行的益处在于能够提高效率并能促进国家间的经济文化交流。

milestone [ˈmailstəun] *n.* 里程碑，划时代的事件

同 landmark *n.* 里程碑，划时代的事件

例 The film proved to be a milestone in the history of cinema. 事实证明这部影片是电影史上的一个里程碑。

tremendous [tri'mendəs] *adj.* 极大的，巨大的；惊人的

同 enormous *adj.* 庞大的

例 In the short time computers have made a tremendous impact on our lives. 在很短的时间里，计算机对我们的生活产生了深远的影响。

keep pace with 跟上，与……并驾齐驱

同 keep up with 跟上……

例 This means that change is not always a personal option, but an inescapable fact of life, and we need to constantly adapt to keep pace with it. 这就意味着改变不总是个人的选择，而是生活中不可避免的现象，我们需要不断地去适应它。

reshape [ˌri:'ʃeip] *vt.* 重塑

拓 shape *vt.* 形成，塑造

例 Television, the most pervasive and persuasive of modern technologies, marked by rapid change and growth, is moving into a new era, an era of extraordinary sophistication and versatility, which promises to reshape our lives and our world.
电视，这项以迅速变化和成长为标志的最普及和最有影响力的现代技术，正在步入一个新时代，一个极为成熟和多元化的时代，这必将重塑我们的生活和世界。

breath-taking [ˌbreθ'teikiŋ] *adj.* 惊人的

同 earth-shattering *adj.* 惊天动地的

例 With the automobile pouring into the world, our way of life has been revolutionized and the society has undergone some breath-taking changes. 随着汽车的诞生，我们的生活发生了变革，社会的发展也发生了翻天覆地的巨变。

incalculable [in'kælkjuləbl] *adj.* 数不清的，不可估量的，极大的

例 TV's influence on the life of the average people is incalculable, including their thoughts, likes and dislikes, even their ways of life. 电视给普通人的生活带来了不可估量的影响，这包括在思维方式、喜好和生活方式等方面。

witness ['witnis] *vt.* 作为……的见证

同 experience *vt.* 经验，经历； undergo *vt.* 经历，经受

例 Technology is now witnessing numerous earth-shaking changes. 科技给人们的生活带来翻天覆地的变化。

dependent [di'pendənt] *adj.* 依靠的，依赖的

用 be dependent on 依赖

例 We are so dependent on computers that it is hard to imagine what things would be like today without them. 我们现在非常依赖电脑，以至于很难想象如果没有电脑生活会变成什么样子。

information explosion 信息爆炸

同 information overload 信息超载

例 Living in such an information explosion era, people can acquire knowledge from different approaches, such as watching TV, surfing the Internet, listening to lectures as well as the distance-learning. 生活在信息爆炸的时代，人们可以通过各种途径来获取知识，如电视、上网、听讲座以及远程学习。

思路拓展

真题范文：互联网

The life will be changing constantly in terms of technology and the Internet is the key to all the knowledge and information available in the world today. 人们的生活因科技而不断地发生变化，互联网是当今世界获得知识和信息的重要来源。

potential [pə'tenʃəl] *n.* 潜能，可能性；*adj.* 潜在的，可能的

同 probability *n.* 可能性； possibility *n.* 可能性

例 They will bring a lot of benefits but they will also increase the potential for unimaginable chaos.
他们带来了许多利益，但也提高了无法设想的混乱的可能性。

inevitability [in,evitə'biləti] *n.* 必然性，不可逃避

拓 inevitable *adj.* 必然的，不可避免的

用 There is a certain inevitability that... 必然会……

例 There is a certain inevitability that technology will progress and become increasingly complex.
科技必然会不断进步，也会日趋复杂。

positively ['pɔzətivli] *adv.* 积极地，正面地

同 beneficial *adj.* 有益的； favorable *adj.* 有利的

例 Medical advances positively help people to live better and longer. 医疗的进步能延长人们的寿命，让人们生活得更好。

negatively ['negətivli] *adv.* 负面地，否定地

同 adversely *adv.* 不利地；banefully *adv.* 有害地
unfavourably *adv.* 不利地

用 answer negatively 否定回答

例 I tend to believe that young children can be negatively affected by spending too much time on the computer every day.
我认为年轻人每天花太多的时间在电脑上可能会产生负面影响。

intense [in'tens] *adj.* 强烈的；紧张的

例 Electronic games tend to be very intense and rather violent.
电子游戏的内容往往很激烈，也相当暴力。

virtual ['vəːtjuəl] *adj.* [计]虚拟的

用 virtual world 虚拟世界；virtual life 虚拟生活
virtual reality 虚拟现实

例 Parents must ensure that their children learn to enjoy other kinds of activity and not simply sit at home, learning to live in a virtual life.
家长必须保证孩子参加各种活动，而不要只待在家里，生活在虚拟的世界里。

思路拓展

真题范文：谈青少年应该活在现实中

Spending time with other children and sharing non-virtual experiences can be an important part of a child's development that cannot be provided by a computer.

unassociated [ˌʌnə'səuʃieitid] *adj.* 无联系的

用 be unassociated with 和……没关系

例 The gap between the poor and the rich is unassociated with technology. Taking advantage of high technology, people can have more chances to make a better living, thus diminish the gap. 贫富之间的差距和科技没有关系。充分利用高科技，人们就能够生活得更好，这样就能缩短贫富差距。

be/become preoccupied with 全神贯注于，沉浸在

用 be/become preoccupied with computer games
沉浸在电脑游戏中

例 As a result, people have become so preoccupied with bits of fragmented information that they pay too little

attention to the larger issues and overall perspectives.
其结果是人们把主要注意力放在七零八碎的信息上，而很少去注意那些更重要的问题和全局。

be addicted to 对……上瘾，沉溺于

同 indulge in 沉溺于

例 Consequently, people are addicted to these activities, totally neglecting the feelings of their family members.
因此，人们对这些活动上瘾，就会完全忽略家人的感受。

addict ['ædikt] *n.* 有瘾的人；*vt.* 使沉溺，使上瘾

拓 addicted *adj.* 上了瘾的；addiction *n.* 上瘾，沉溺
addictive *adj.* 上瘾的

用 Internet addict 有网瘾的人
video-game addict 对电脑游戏上瘾的人
addict oneself to 沉溺于，醉心于

例 When children become computer game addict, they will live a sedentary life.
当儿童对游戏上瘾时，就会久坐不动。

posture ['pɔstʃə] *n.* 姿势，姿态；*vt.* 做出某种姿势

例 This is partly because sitting in front of a screen for too long can be damaging to both the eyes and the physical posture of children, regardless of what they are using the computer for.
部分原因在于无论孩子用电脑做什么，在屏幕前坐得太久会对他们的视力和身形有害。

overweight [ˌəuvə'weit] *adj.* 超重的，过重的；*n.* 超重

例 There is plenty of evidence to suggest that children are overweight and the situation is getting worse, according to the medical experts. 据医学专家称，

他们有足够的证据表明现在的孩子身体超重，而且这种情况持续恶化。

undermine [ˌʌndəˈmain] *vt.* 破坏，渐渐破坏

同 destroy *vt.* 破坏； sabotage *vt.* 蓄意破坏

用 much exposure to…would undermine…
接触……过多会损害……

undermine the personal growth physically and mentally
影响身心发育

例 Much exposure to undesirable information on the Internet or the mass media would undermine the personal growth of children physically and mentally.
孩子通过互联网或媒体接触过多的不良信息会对他们的身心发育产生不良的影响。

assertive [əˈsəːtiv] *adj.* 武断的

例 Adult video gamers also seemed less outgoing, or extroverted, and less social and assertive than non-gamers, leading sedentary life, having weight issues and mental health concerns.
玩游戏的成年人不愿意进行户外活动、内向、不善于与人交际、武断，过着久坐不动的生活。他们身心都不健康。

be obsessed with 着迷于

同 indulge in 沉溺于；be addicted to 沉溺于

例 Common complaints found among children who are obsessed with games are eye strains, wrist, neck and back pains, etc.
沉迷于游戏的孩子常常抱怨眼疲劳，手腕、脖子和背部疼痛等。

思路拓展

computer games

电脑游戏玩家更愿意多花时间玩游戏，沉迷于虚拟的世界(indulge in the virtual life)，而不是走到外面(outdoor activities)，和真实的世界打交道。

exposure [iks'pəuʒə] *n.* 暴露；接触

拓 expose *vt.* 使暴露，使显露 (to)

用 exposure to… 接触（名词）

例 The player is usually the "hero" of the game and too much exposure can encourage children to be self-centered and insensitive to others. 玩家通常是游戏中的"英雄"，经常玩游戏的孩子容易以自我为中心，并且对外界很敏感。

gadget ['gædʒit] *n.* 小玩意，小器具

例 People are skilled at using their thumbs to manipulate objects such as mobile phone keys, small joysticks, notebook computer pointers and any gadget with the thumb acting on the keypad. 人们都能够熟练地用他们的拇指操作手机键盘、游戏杆、笔记本电脑指示钮以及任何可以用拇指操作键盘的仪器。

alienation [ˌeiliə'neiʃən] *n.*（感情上的）疏远，冷漠

拓 alienate *vt.* 使疏远，离间； alienated *adj.* 疏远的

用 alienation between family members 家人关系疏远

例 People tend to be so dependent on TV that they fail to communicate with other family members, which in turn, will cause the generation gap, alienation between family members and other social problems. 人们容易过度依赖电视，以至于不爱和家人交流，那么就会导致代沟、感情疏远及其他社会问题。

geographically [ˌdʒiəˈgræfikəli] *adv.* 在地理上；地理学上

例 Many people hold the view that mobile phone is of great significance in maintaining their relationship while geographically separated. 很多人认为尽管有地域的阻隔，手机仍能维持人们之间的关系。

telecommunication [ˈtelikəˌmjuniˈkeiʃən] *n.* 远程通讯

例 The various technologies that can be used for the purpose of telecommunication are mobile phones, satellite phones, radios, televisions and networks. 手机、卫星电话、广播、电视及网络都可以用于远程通讯。

substitute [ˈsʌbstitjuːt] *n.* 代替者，代用品；*vi.&vt.* 代替

拓 substitutable *adj.* 可替换的

substituted *adj.* 取代的，代替的

同 replace *vt.* 取代，代替

用 it is no substitute for… 无法替代……

例 Even when children use a computer for other purposes, such as getting information or emailing friends, it is no substitute for human interaction. 即使孩子们使用电脑是为了其他目的，例如获取信息或发邮件给朋友，那也无法替代人与人之间的直接交流。

overuse [ˌəuvəˈjuːz] *n.* 使用过度；*vt.* 过度使用

用 overuse natural resources 过度使用自然资源

例 I think the main point is to make sure that young children do not overuse computers. 我认为关键的一点是要保证孩子不要过度地使用电脑。

keep alive 保持生机

例 Interestingly, technology can positively contribute to keeping alive of traditional skills and ways of life. 有趣的是，科技有助于提高传统技术水平，改变

生活方式，使生活充满生机和活力。

access to 接近，通向……的入口；有权使用

同 entry *n.* 进入，入口；approach *n.* 方法，接近

用 have/gain access to 使用；接触

remote access 远程访问

例 Mobile phones give us the instant access to information. 手机能让我们收到即时信息。

text [tekst] *vt.* 发短信

同 send short messages 发短信

例 From making a phone call to texting, and now internet access for just a touch of your finger tips, mobile phones are shaping our life. 从打电话到发短信，再到现在手指轻轻一按便可上网，手机改变着我们的生活。

keep track of 记录；了解……的动态；留心……的发展

用 keep track of time 掌控时间

例 Parents need to keep track of how much time their children spend in front of the screen playing games and also as to what type of games they play. 家长要留心孩子玩游戏玩了多长时间及他们玩什么样的游戏。

maintain a balance 维持平衡

例 Every aspect has its advantages and disadvantages; so is the law of nature. What we can do is try to maintain a balance and get the best of what it has to offer, be it nature or technology. 任何事物都具有优劣势，自然规律亦是如此。无论是对自然还是对科技，我们能做到的就是努力保持平衡，取其精华。

selective [si'lektiv] *adj.* 选择的

例 We must realize that television itself is neither good nor bad, and its values in the modern world depend on how it is used. The best solution, in my opinion, is

to be selective, not to indulge in it.
我们要认识到电视本身无好坏之分，它的价值取决于在现代社会你如何使用它。我认为最好的方法就是看电视要有选择性，而不要沉迷其中。

get a hold of 找到；与……联系（或接触）

例 Whenever they go online, people immediately get a hold of best-selling books, popular music and prevailing TV shows. 无论何时，人们上网都能找到畅销的书籍、流行的音乐和受欢迎的电视节目。

链接机经关键词

- Internet跟上科学的发展(keep pace with scientific advances)

  随着因特网技术出现(with the advent of the Internet technology)，全球信息化(global information)及信息高速公路(the information superhighway)进入人们的视线。许多科技的创新(innovation)，例如，交流工具(communication tool)、电信(telecommunication)等，重新塑造了我们的生活(reshape our life)，改变了我们的生活方式。通讯工具具有方便快捷(convenient and efficient)的特点，它在帮助人们处理紧急事情(deal with emergencies)、加快生活节奏(accelerate/speed up the pace of life)的同时拉近了人们之间的距离(shorten the distance between people)。

- mobile phone

  手机作为现代化的交流工具(communication tool)能够使人与人的交往(communicate with others)克服地域的障碍(overcome geographical barrier)，但是这会引起人们过度依赖手机的现象(overly-dependent on mobile phones)。

- **television**

  电视不但提供有趣的(interesting)、有教育意义的(instructive)节目，而且使我们消息灵通(keep us informed)。我们能从电视中了解到的资讯有：
  最新的国内外消息(the latest news at home and abroad)；
  大量的电视报道(massive television coverage)；
  休闲娱乐信息(entertainment)。

- **computer**

  由于计算机强大的功能(marvelous functions)和准确性(accuracy)，使用它能使人们快速地完成任务(accomplish the task fast)，提高工作效率(achieve the high efficiency)。

3. 环境题材

考点回顾

20130309	减少飞机旅行是最好的环保方式
20091031	环境问题个人还是政府解决
20090711	谁来承担污染处理费用
20090221	个人解决环境问题
20090212	科技解决环境问题
20050806	环境污染中的垃圾问题

environment [in'vaiərənmənt] *n.* 环境，自然环境

拓 environmental *adj.* 环境的
environmentally *adv.* 有关环境方面
environmentalism *n.* 环境保护论

environmentalist *n.* 环保主义者

用 ruin the environment 破坏环境

protect the environment from the pollution
保护环境不受污染

例 Economic development is clearly essential for communities' livelihoods and the well-being of nations, but is often a source of harmful pollution to the environment. 很显然，经济发展有利于国富民强，但同时也是环境污染的源头。

思路拓展

环保4R的理念

Reduction 减量	Reuse 重复使用
Recycling 回收	Regeneration 再生

pollution [pə'luʃən] *n.* 污染

拓 pollute *vt.* 污染

polluted *adj.* 受污染的

pollutant *n.* 污染物

organic pollutants 有机污染物

white pollution 白色污染

同 contamination *n.* 污染，污染物

例 People would pay high price for the environmental pollution caused by man-made waste. 人们会为自身产生的垃圾所造成的环境污染付出高昂的代价。

contaminate [kən'tæmineit] *vt.* 污染

拓 contamination *n.* 污染，污染物

contaminant *n.* 污染物，致污物

同 pollute *vt.* 污染

例 Environmental pollutants from many different sources contaminate water, air, and land, putting humans and ecosystems at risk. 不同来源的环境污染物会污染水、空气及土壤，使人类和生态系统面临威胁。

alleviate [ə'li:vieit] *vt.* 减轻，缓和

用 alleviate burdens 减负；alleviate pressure 减压

例 One thing is for sure, that by using more energy efficient, we will be helping to alleviate the toll on environment and human health.
可以确定的一点是，通过使用更节约的能源，我们将会减少在环境和健康方面付出的代价。

at the expense of 以……为代价

同 at the cost of 以……为代价

例 He finished the job at the expense of his health.
他完成了那件工作，但却损害了健康。

waste [weist] *n.* 废物；浪费

同 refuse *n.* 垃圾，废物；garbage *n.* 垃圾，废物
rubbish *n.* 垃圾，废物

例 I think it is true that in almost every country today each household and family produces a large amount of waste every week. 我认为今天几乎在所有的国家，家家户户每周都要产生大量的垃圾。

ecological [ˌi:kə'lɔdʒikəl] *adj.* 生态的，生态学的

拓 ecology *n.* 生态学

用 ecological balance/equilibrium 生态平衡

例 It is no doubt that animals play a vital role in maintaining the ecological equilibrium. 毫无疑问，动物在维持生态平衡方面起着至关重要的作用。

ecosystem ['i:kəusistəm] *n.* 生态系统

例 There are highly sensitive and delicately balanced ecosystems in the forest.

森林里有高度敏感、灵敏平衡的各种生态系统。

worsen ['wə:sn] *vi.&vt.* 恶化，变得更坏

拓 worse *adj.* 更坏的，更差的

worsening *adj.* 日益恶化的

同 deteriorate *vi.&vt.* 恶化

例 Already low living standards have been worsened by stringent economic reforms. 严峻的经济改革使本已很低的生活水平愈加恶化。

extinction [iks'tiŋkʃən] *n.* 消灭，消失，灭绝

拓 extinct *adj.* 灭绝的，绝种的

同 extermination *n.* 消灭，灭绝

用 the mass extinction of… ……大规模灭绝

例 The plant is now in danger of extinction.

这种植物正濒临灭绝。

sewage ['sju:idʒ] *n.* 污水，污物

同 drainage *n.* 排水，污水

用 sewage disposal/treatment 污水处理

sewage purification 污水净化

sewage utilization 污水利用

例 This city needs a new sewage disposal system.

这座城市需要一套新的污水处理系统。

disposable [dis'pəuzəbl] *adj.* 一次性使用的

拓 dispose *vt.&vi.* 处理，处置

例 The use of disposable products had led to a marked increase in trash.

由于使用一次性的物品导致了垃圾明显增多。

harness ['hɑ:nis] *vt.* 利用

同 utilise *vt.* 利用；make use of 利用

take advantage of 利用

用 harness the solar energy 利用太阳能

例 Scientists have known how to harness the limitless power of the sun.
科学家已知道如何利用有限的太阳能。

eliminate [i'limineit] *vt.* 消除，排除

拓 elimination *n.* 消除；淘汰

同 exclude *vt.* 排除； remove *vt.* 去掉，消除

用 eliminate noises 消除噪声
eliminate poverty 消除贫困
eliminate illiteracy 扫盲

例 In line with a growing international trend on the use of plastic bags, many governments have experimented with heavy taxes, outright bans or eliminating the thinnest bags.
为了与国际接轨，很多政府在使用塑料袋的问题上，尝试征税、明令禁止或是取消使用。

ruin ['ruin] *vt.* 破坏，毁掉

同 damage *vt.&vi.* 损害，损毁；destroy *vt.* 破坏

用 ruin the environment 破坏环境

例 Many human activities can ruin the environment and some are even irreversible. 人类的很多行为都可能破坏环境，甚至有些无法挽回。

biodegradable [,baiəudi'greidəbl] *adj.* 生物所能分解的，能进行生物降解的

拓 degrade *vt.* 使……降解；*vi.* 退化
degradable *adj.* 可能降解的

用 biodegradable garbage 可生物降解的垃圾

例 Biodegradable plastic as a novel material possesses a vast range of application prospect. 生物降解塑料作为一种新型材料，有很好的应用前景。

exhaust [ig'zɔ:st] *vt.* 耗尽；排出；*n.* 废气

拓 exhausted *adj.* 耗尽的；exhaustion *n.* 枯竭，耗尽

同 use up 用完，耗尽； consume *vt.* 消耗

用 air exhaust 排气

motor vehicle exhaust 汽车尾气排放

例 Motor vehicle exhaust leads partly to the greenhouse effect. 机动车尾气排放是导致温室效应的部分原因。

be in short supply 供应不足

拓 water shortage 水资源短缺

run out of resources 资源短缺

同 shortage *n.* 缺乏，缺少；scarcity *n.* 不足，缺乏

lack of 缺乏

例 It is widely-accepted that water as a valuable resource is in short supply in some areas. 众所周知，水作为一种珍贵的资源，在某些地区供应不足。

ozone layer 臭氧层

例 Pollution leads to depletion of the ozone layer, global warming and climate change. 污染导致臭氧层的空洞，全球变暖及气候变化。

use up 用完，耗尽

例 Certainly nobody wants to see our resources used up and our planet poisoned by waste.

当然，没人愿意看到资源用尽、地球遍地垃圾。

consume [kən'sju:m] *vt.* 消耗，消费

例 The reason why we have so much packaging is that we consume so much more on a daily basis than the families did in the past.

我们之所以能用掉大量的包装袋，其原因在于现在每日包装袋的消耗量要比过去大得多。

discharge [dis'tʃɑ:dʒ] *vt.* 流出，放出；排出

例 The wound is still discharging pus. 伤口仍在流脓。

release [ri'li:s] *vt.* 释放，发射；*n.* 释放

例 Air pollution is caused by the release of chemicals and particles into the atmosphere. 空气污染是由于化学物质释放到大气中而造成的。

emission [i'miʃən] *n.* 排放，散发，发出（气体、光、热）

拓 emit *vt.* 发出，散发（光、热、声音、气等）

用 the emission of… 排放……

emission reduction 减排

carbon emission reduction 碳减排

例 The restriction of the number of cars can reduce greenhouse gas emissions to a large extent. 从很大程度上来说，限制车的数量可以减少温室气体的排放。

zero-emission ['ziərəu,i'miʃn] *n.* 零排放

例 In addition to public transport, switching to zero-emission vehicles is another approach to control the air pollution in major cities. 除了提高公共交通外，改用零排放的车辆是很多大城市控制空气污染的另一个方法。

exploitation [,eksplɔi'teiʃən] *n.* 剥削，榨取；开发，开采

拓 exploit *vt.* 开发，开拓；over-exploitation *n.* 过度开采

例 It is an unfortunate fact that many employers may prefer to use the services of children simply to save money by paying them less than adults and it is this type of exploitation that should be discouraged.
不幸的是很多雇主愿意雇用童工，因为付给他们的薪水要比付给成年人的低很多，我们应该阻止这种剥削行为。

hazardous ['hæzədəs] *adj.*（化合物）有害的，危险的

拓 hazard *vt.* 使遭受危险；*n.* 危险

同 poisonous *adj.* 有毒的，有害的

dangerous *adj.* 危险的

用 hazardous material 有害物质

例 The situation has the potential to be hazardous, but no people, property, or environment is currently affected by this. 这种情况可能很危险，但是人、财产及环境目前不会受到影响。

degradation [ˌdegrə'deiʃən] *n.* 退化，恶化

拓 degrade *vt.* 使……降解；*vi.* 退化

degradable *adj.* 可能降解的

用 environmental degradation 环境恶化

例 Grassland degradation has become one of the prominent environmental problems in this area. 草地退化已成为这一地区突出的环境问题之一。

deforestation [diˌfɔris'teiʃən] *n.* 森林砍伐

拓 deforest *vt.* 采伐森林

反 afforestation *n.* 造林

例 The main cause of soil erosion is deforestation for farmland reclamation. 水土流失的主要原因是毁林开荒。

思路拓展

Disregard or ignorance of intrinsic value（内在规律）, lax forest management（松散的森林管理） and deficient environmental law（不严格的环境保护法） are some of the factors that allow deforestation to occur on a large scale（大规模的森林砍伐）. In many countries, deforestation is an ongoing issue that is causing extinction（灭绝）, changes to climatic conditions（气候条件）, desertification（土壤沙漠化）, and displacement of indigenous people（本土居民的迁移）.

renewable [ri'njuəbl] *adj.* 可更新的；可继续的；可再生的

拓 renew *vt.&vi.*（使）复原；（使）更新

用 renewable energy 可再生能源

non-renewable resource不可再生资源

例 A government-sponsored renewable energy project will be launched next month.

政府资助的可再生能源项目将于下个月启动。

pose a threat to 对……构成威胁

例 If people still pose a threat to natural habitats, then natural resources will be depleted and environment will be degraded. 如果人们仍然威胁动物的自然栖息地，那么自然资源将会枯竭，环境将恶化。

vulnerable ['vʌlnərəbl] *adj.* 有弱点的，易受伤害的

例 The potato is vulnerable to pests.

马铃薯易受害虫的侵害。

deterioration [di,tiəriə'reiʃən] *n.* 恶化，退化

反 amelioration *n.* 改进，改善

用 climatic deterioration 气候恶化

例 The deterioration of the biological environment, caused by rapid economic development and population growth, has harmed the biological diversity and threatened the sustainable development.

经济的快速发展及人口的迅速膨胀导致了生态环境的恶化，破坏了生物多样性并对可持续发展造成了威胁。

fossil fuels 矿物燃料

例 There is a growing concern regarding the collaboration between fossil fuels and environmental pollution.

人们越来越关注矿物燃料和环境污染之间的关系。

真题再现

Fossil fuels, such as coal, oil, natural gas, are used in many countries, but in some countries, the use of alternative sources of energy, including wind and solar power, are encouraged. Is this trend a positive or a negative development? (20090530)

关键词解读：记得在一部美国影片中：一位年轻人指着不远处的一个老头，对其伙伴说：Hey , look at that fossil fuel. 这里的fossil fuel是指“老不死的”。那么这道雅思作文里的关键词fossil fuel，指的是化石燃料，包括煤炭、石油、天然气等在特定地质条件下形成的沉积矿石。non-fossil fuel 指的就是非矿物燃料。

irreversible [ˌiri'vəːsəbl] *adj.* 不可逆的，不可挽回的

拓 reverse *vt.* 颠倒，倒转

同 irreparable *adj.* 不能挽回的，不能修补的

用 irreversible change 不可逆变化

irreversible process 不可逆过程

例 New economy and globalization have become an unavoidable fact and an irreversible trend. 新经济全球化已是无法回避的事实，而且趋势不可逆转。

packaging ['pækidʒing] *n.* 包装

例 Most of this rubbish comes from the packaging from the things we buy, such as processed food.

大量的垃圾来自于我们购买商品的包装，例如，加工食品等。

throw away 扔掉，丢弃

例 However, the amount of waste produced is also a result of our tendency to use something once and throw it away. 然而，大量垃圾的产生也是由于我们越来越多地使用一次性产品然后就扔掉的结果。

dispose of 处理，解决

例 We also think that it is a source of pollution and difficult to dispose of.
我们也认为这是污染的源头，很难处理掉。

put the blame on 把责任归咎于……

例 It is reasonable to put the blame on the human's inadequate manners as for the worsening environment.
关于环境的恶化，把责任都归咎于人们不当的行为是合理的。

blameworthy ['bleim,wə:ði] *adj.* 该受责备的，应受谴责的

同 blameful *adj.* 应受责备的，该受谴责的
reprehensible *adj.* 应斥责的，应该谴责的
blamable *adj.* 可责备的；有过失的
culpable *adj.* 应受责备的，应受处罚的

例 If one litters randomly, then he will be blameworthy for lack of awareness of environmental protection. 如果有人随处扔垃圾，将因缺乏环保意识受到谴责。

degrade [di'greid] *vt.* 使退化

例 Due to the pressures of population and our technology, the environment is being degraded.
由于人口和科技产生的压力，环境正在恶化。

address [ə'dres] *vt.* 设法解决，满足（需求），处理

同 tackle *vt.* 处理；solve *vt.* 解决；handle *vt.* 处理

用 address environmental problems 解决环境问题
address the need of... 满足……的需要

例 Only when the government, society and every family make joint efforts, will we begin to address the environmental pollution. 只有政府、社会和每个家庭共同努力才能解决环境污染问题。

take action 采取行动

拓 take measures 采取措施

例 Children can be educated about environmental issues at school, but adults need to take action.
学校要向孩子们普及环境保护知识，但家长也要身体力行。

enforcement [in'fɔːsmənt] *n.* 执行，实施

拓 enforce *vt.* 实施

例 Populations in developing countries are especially at risk because of often inadequate knowledge, lack of appropriate regulation and enforcement as well as barriers to accessing "cleaner" technologies. 由于知识缺乏，没有相关的法规及实施以及接触不到环保方面的科技，发展中国家的人处于危境之中。

life-sustaining [laifˌsə'steiniŋ] *adj.* 维系生命的

例 Water is life-sustaining, however, it is contaminated by the pollutants discharged by the chemical factories.
水是生命之源，然而却受到化工厂排出的污染物的污染。

preserve [pri'zəːv] *vt.* 保存，保护

拓 preservation *n.* 保存，保护

同 protect *vt.* 保护； conserve *vt.* 保护，保藏

例 It is the compelling responsibility of both the government and individual to preserve the environment.
保护环境是政府和个人不可推卸的责任。

alternative [ɔːl'təːnətiv] *adj.* 选择性的；交替的；*n.* 可供选择的事物

同 substitute *n.* 代用品，代替者
replacement *n.* 代替者

用 alternative energy 替代能源；新能源

例 Solar energy is the most abundant source of energy on Earth, which is the fastest growing type of alternative energy. 太阳能资源极为丰富，是发展迅速的可替代能源。

launch [lɔ:ntʃ] *vt.* 开展（活动、计划等）

同 start *vt.* 开始，启动

用 launch a crackdown on plastic bags
发起限用塑料袋活动
launch a programme 启动一个项目

例 The long-term protection launched by the government will provide comprehensive and systematic support for biological diversity protection.
政府启动的长期保护方案将会为物种多样性的保护提供全面而系统的支持。

make concerted effort 携手解决，齐心协力

同 make joint efforts 共同努力

例 People should make concerted efforts in order to tackle the problem of water scarcity.
人们应该齐心协力共同解决水资源短缺问题。

sustainable [sə'steinəbl] *adj.* 可持续的

拓 sustain *vt.* 维持，支撑；sustaining *adj.* 持续的
sustainability *n.* 持续性

用 sustainable agriculture 可持续农业

例 Sustainable development is the common target of human beings. 可持续发展是人类追求的共同目标。

low carbon 低碳

用 low-carbon economy 低碳经济
low-carbon technology 低碳科技

例 How to live a low carbon life is a hot topic in both developing and developed countries.
怎样才是低碳生活在发展中国家和发达国家都是一个热门话题。

背景文化

低碳，英文为low carbon，意指较低（更低）的温室气体（二氧化碳为主）排放。Low-carbon refers to a minimal output of greenhouse gas emissions into the biosphere, specifically refers to the greenhouse gas carbon dioxide。随着世界工业经济的发展、人口的剧增、人类欲望的无限上升和生产生活方式的无节制，世界气候面临越来越严重的问题，二氧化碳排放量越来越大，地球臭氧层正遭受前所未有的危机，全球灾难性气候变化屡屡出现，已经严重危害到人类的生存环境和健康安全。

carbon footprint 碳足迹

例 Green construction techniques contribute to a reduced carbon footprint. 绿色建筑技术有助于减少碳足迹。

背景拓展

carbon footprint（碳足迹）是《韦氏大词典》2009年度新添加的词汇，碳足迹是用来标示一个人或者团体的“碳耗用量”。“碳”，就是石油、煤炭、木材等由碳元素构成的自然资源。“碳”耗用得多，导致地球变暖的元凶“二氧化碳”也制造得多，“碳足迹”相应的就大，反之“碳足迹”就小。总的来说“碳足迹”就是指一个人的能源意识和行为对自然界产生的影响。

biodiversity [ˌbaiəudaiˈvəːsəti] *n.* 生物多样性

同 biological diversity 生物多样性

例 The findings have broader relevance to the protection and restoration of biodiversity. 研究发现保护生物多样性与恢复生物多样性的关系很大。

renewable [ri'njuəbl] *adj.* 可更新的，可继续的，可再生的

用 renewable resources 可再生资源

例 Many countries take firm actions to increase the efficiency of energy resources, develop the renewable resources and reduce greenhouse gas emission.
很多国家采取措施来提高能源的使用效率，开发再生能源及减少温室气体排放量。

enact relevant laws 制定相关立法

例 It is the compelling obligation of government to enact relevant laws to safeguard the environment. 制定相关法律来保护环境是政府不可推卸的责任。

give prominence to 突出，重视

同 give priority to 优先考虑

例 Government would give prominence to buildings a resource-conserving, environment-friendly society in its strategy of industrialization and modernization.
在工业化和现代化的战略中，政府应该注重建设资源节约型、环境友好型社会。

attach great importance to 重视

同 pay attention to 注意，重视
take sth. seriously 严肃对待

例 Government attaches great importance to environmental protection and regards it as highly significant in the realization of sustainable development.
政府要高度重视环保，这对实现可持续发展至关重要。

place restraints on 限制

同 impose restrictions on 限制

例 Governments began placing restraints on activities that caused environmental degradation.

政府开始限制人们破坏环境的行为。

implement ['implimənt] *vt.* 实现，使生效，实施

例 All laws and regulations against the pollution should be forcefully implemented.
应该坚决实施与环境污染相关的法律法规。

harsh [hɑ:ʃ] *adj.* 严厉的，严酷的

同 strict *adj.* 严格的
severe *adj.* 严峻的，严厉的

用 take stronger and harsher measures
采取更强有力的措施

例 Harsher measures should be taken so as to combat the worsening environment pollution. 应该采取更严厉的措施来解决日益恶化的环境污染。

urge [ə:dʒ] *vt.* 力劝，催促；*vi.* 强烈要求

例 Rubbish collectors were urged to separate plastic for reprocessing and cut the amount burned or buried.
塑料应与垃圾分开，进行再加工，而且要减少对其燃烧和填埋。

on...level 在……层次上

例 Environmental protection should be carried out on individual, organizational or governmental level, for the benefit of the natural environment and humans.
为了自然环境和人类，个人、组织及政府各个方面都要为保护环境而努力。

environmental engineering 环境工程

例 Academic institutions now offer courses such as environmental studies, environmental management and environmental engineering that study the history and methods of environmental protection.

学校开设像环境研究，环境管理及环境工程等课程来研究环境保护的历史及方法。

safeguard ['seifgɑ:d] *vt.* 保护，护卫

用 safeguard the ecosystem 保护生态系统

例 If everyone has the awareness of safeguarding the ecosystem, the environment will change for better.
如果每个人都有保护生态系统的意识，这样环境将会改善。

recycle [ˌri:'saikl] *vt.* 使再循环，使……重新利用；*vi.* 重复利用

例 Governments can encourage such action by putting taxes on packaging, such as plastic bags, by providing recycling services and by fining households and shops that do not attempt to recycle their waste.
政府应该通过对包装征税，如对塑料袋征税，提供再循环使用的服务及对废物不进行循环使用的家庭和商店进行罚款来鼓励这种行为。

translate...into 转化，转变为

例 Researchers should develop sustainable solutions to help translate research findings into action.
研究者应该找到持久的解决方法，将科研成果应用到实际中。

consciousness ['kɔnʃəsnis] *n.* 意识

拓 conscious *adj.* 意识到的
unconscious *adj.* 无意识的

同 awareness *n.* 意识，认识

用 raise environmental consciousness among the general public 提高全民环保意识
environmental protection consciousness 环保意识

例 I think, therefore, that government needs to raise this consciousness in the general public.
因此，我认为政府应该提升大众的意识。

写作提示

表示"提高、加强"的意识常用动词有：raise/ enhance/ boost/cultivate。

environmentally-friendly [in'vairənmentli,frendli]
adj. 环保的

同 eco-friendly *adj.* 生态友好的，对环境无害的

用 environmentally-friendly policy 环保政策

例 People should cultivate the sense of using environmentally-friendly product in daily life.
人们在日常生活中应该养成使用环保产品的习惯。

写作提示

解决环境污染的途径有：
utilise the natural resources properly
合理利用自然资源（政府）
adopt environmentally-friendly policy
采取环保政策（政府）

individual efforts 个人努力

例 Environmental protection involves the international cooperation as well as individual efforts.
环境保护需要国际合作，也需要每个人的努力。

链接机经关键词

⊙ 污染

环境污染(pollution/contamination)日益严重(worsening)，对生态系统的平衡(ecological balance)造成

了威胁(pose a threat to)，如汽车带来的尾气排放(emission of cars)造成了空气污染、温室气体(greenhouse gas)带来了全球变暖(climate change)。

- 原因

人口爆炸

overpopulation→scarcity of water→inadequate behaviours

- 过度工业化

over-industrialization→use up the resources→ignore sustainable development

- 过度开发

overexploitation→consume the natural resources and threaten the equilibrium of ecosystem

- 解决方案

意识提升：enhance the awareness of environmental protection of the general public

再度利用：reuse/recycle/renewable/reproduce

加强保护：strengthen the preservation

全面合作：government, society and every family make joint efforts, involve the international cooperation as well as individuals' effort

开发能源：explore alternative energy to replace the fossil fuels
explore environmentally-friendly fuels

采取措施：take harsher measures

出台法律：enact the relevant laws
work out the regulations

普及教育：popularize the knowledge of environmental protection, cultivate the good habit in life

倡导媒体：arouse the public's attention to the importance of environment

4 工作题材

考点回顾

A类题目
20130110 工作满意度与人生的意义
20100415 女性的职业
20091203 兼职与全职

G类题目
20090905 学生做兼职
20090613 经常换工作

career [kə'riə] *n.* 事业，职业

同 occupation *n.* 职业；profession *n.* 职业，专业
vocation *n.* 职业，天职

用 career choice 职业选择
career counseling 职业咨询
career development 职业发展
career objective 职业目标
career path 职业道路
career planning 职业生涯规划
career prospects 职业前程

例 Competition is constant and a player is tested every time they perform in their relatively short career. 在相对短暂的职业生涯中，运动员面临着不断的竞争及考验。

profession [prə'feʃən] *n.* 职业，专业

拓 professional *adj.* 专业的，职业的；*n.* 专业人员

professionally *adv.* 专业地，内行地

用 all professions and trades 各行各业

例 However, it is also true that it is only those who reach the very top of their profession can get their huge salaries. 然而也只有那些达到事业顶峰的人才能获得高薪回报。

professional [prəˈfeʃənəl] *n.* 职业运动员，专业人员

例 As a result of constant media attention, sports professionals in my country have become stars, and those at the top are paid huge salaries.
由于媒体的不断关注，在我们国家，职业运动员成了明星，那些优秀运动员的薪酬丰厚。

full-time job 全职工作

拓 job-hunting 求职；job-hunter 求职者
job-seeker 求职者；job vacancy 职位空缺
job satisfaction 工作满足感

同 full-time employment 全职工作

例 Nowadays many adults have full-time jobs and the proportion of their lives spent on such jobs is very high.
现在很多人都拥有一份全职工作，而且大部分时间也都花在了这份工作上。

part-time job 兼职工作

同 moonlight *vi.* （尤指在夜间）从事第二职业

例 A proper part-time job does not occupy students' too much time. 一份适当的兼职工作并不会占用学生太多的时间。

earn one's fortune 谋生

同 make a living 谋生

例 Teachers, nurses, laboratory researchers, etc. are never listed among the best-paid professionals, yet they are more important to our well-being and our future than the stars who earn their fortunes so quickly. 教师、护士及研究员都不在高薪行列之内，但是与那些高薪的明星相比，他们对我们的幸福生活和未来更重要。

remunerative [ri'mju:nərətiv] *adj.* 有报酬的，有利可图的

拓 remunerate *vt.* 酬劳； remuneration *n.* 报酬

同 profitable *adj.* 有利可图的，赚钱的

fruitful *adj.* 有收获的，有利的

例 It is necessary to decide between remunerative work and meaningful work. 在一份高薪的工作和一份有价值的工作间做出抉择是很有必要的。

probation [prə'beiʃən] *n.* 试用，见习

拓 probationer *n.* 试用人员，实习生

用 probation period 试用期； on probation 作为试用

例 There is a three-month period of probation for new recruits. 新入职的员工有三个月试用期。

employee [im'plɔii:] *n.* 雇员

拓 employment *n.* 雇用

unemployment *n.* 失业

self-employed *adj.* 自己经营的

例 Employees get job satisfaction in a number of ways. Firstly, a person needs to feel that they are doing valued and valuable work, so positive feedback from superiors is very important in this respect. 职员可以从很多方面获得对工作的满足感。首先，每个人都需要感受到他们正在做有价值并被认可的工作。因此，从这方面来讲，从上级那里得到的良好反馈很重要。

out of work 失业的

同 unemployed *adj.* 失业的

jobless *adj.* 失业的

例 The recession has put millions out of work.
这次经济衰退使数百万人失业。

背景知识

学生毕业后找不到工作的原因：

（1）新毕业生（newly graduated students）缺少工作经验（lack of experience），所以在人才市场上（talent market）就没有竞争优势（less competitive）；

（2）大部分的学生对自己的求职目标期望过高（high expectation of career）；

（3）另外人才的供需不平衡也是造成很难找到工作的原因（the imbalance of supply and demand in the labor market）。

sensitive ['sensitiv] *adj.* 敏感的

用 be sensitive to 对……敏感

例 The issue of children doing paid work is a complex and sensitive one. 孩子干活是否应付钱，这是一个既复杂又敏感的话题。

varying ['veəriŋ] *adj.* 变化的，不同的

拓 vary *vi.* 变化；*vt.* 改变
various *adj.* 各种各样的
variety *n.* 多样
variation *n.* 变化

例 Opinions will also differ as to "learning" benefits; no doubt teachers and factory owner, for example, would have varying concerns.
关于是否会学到一些技能，观点有所不同。难怪老师和工厂老板有不同的关注点。

undertake [ˌʌndə'teik] *vt.* 承担，保证；从事

用 undertake the due obligations 承担应有的义务

例 An important consideration is the kind of work

undertaken. 要着重考虑所从事的工作的性质。

additional [ə'diʃənəl] *adj.* 附加的，额外的

同 extra *adj.* 额外的

例 However, in many countries children work because their families need the additional income, no matter how small.
然而，很多国家的孩子出去工作就是因为能给家里带来一些额外的收入，不管收入有多么的微薄。

judge [dʒʌdʒ] *vt.* 判断

拓 judgment *n.* 判断，裁判

例 This was certainly the case in the past in many industrialized countries, and it is very difficult to judge if it is wrong for children today to contribute to the family income in this way. 过去很多工业化的国家也是如此，今天仍然很难判断孩子们通过这种方式来为家里赚钱是否正确。

over paid 收入过高

同 well-paid *adj.* 待遇优厚的，收入高的

例 I agree with the view that stars in the entertainment business are usually over paid.
我同意娱乐明星收入过高的这种说法。

hold top position 事业达到顶峰

拓 present position 目前的职位
current position 当前的岗位
hold the position 所在职位
be promoted to a higher position 升职

同 reach the very top of the profession 达到职业顶峰

例 Furthermore, the majority of stars do not hold their top positions long.
此外，大部分明星的巅峰时期都不会很长。

be replaced by 替代

同 take the place of 代替

例 Sport stars and pop stars, for example, are soon replaced by the next younger, more energetic, generation, while the good looks of most film stars quickly fade. 体育明星及流行歌手，很快就会被年轻又活力四射的新生代所取代，而电影明星的光环也会很快就消退。

make a contribution to 做出贡献

同 contribute to 有助于

例 Unfortunately, professionals from other fields, who make a much greater contribution to human society, are paid so much less that it is hard to disagree with the statement. 遗憾的是，其他行业的专业人员也为社会做出了巨大的贡献，而收入却微不足道，他们就很难认同这一观点。

for the good of 为了……的好处，为了……的利益

例 The gaps between the stars' earnings and those of people who work less selfishly for the good of society cannot be justified. 明星与那些无私地为社会做出贡献的人之间存在的收入差距是不合理的。

monotonous [mə'nɔtənəs] *adj.* 单调的

例 Job hopping means a broad range of work and life experience rather than the monotonous life. 跳槽意味着不断地充实自己的生活和工作经历，而不是单调乏味的生活。

reward [ri'wɔ:d] *n.* 报酬，报答，奖赏

拓 rewarding *adj.* 值得的，有报酬的

rewardful *adj.* 有报酬的

rewardless *adj.* 徒劳的，无报酬的

同 payment *n.* 付款，报酬

用 reward for 作为……的回报

reward sb. for sth. 由于某事奖赏某人

reward and punishment 奖惩

financial reward 经济回报

例 Many people find sports professionals' rewards unfair, especially when comparing these super salaries with those of top surgeons or research scientists, or even leading politicians who have the responsibility of governing the country. 很多人觉得职业运动员的高额收入不公平，尤其当把他们的高薪和优秀的医生或科学家的收入相对比时，或者和拥有治理国家的出色政治家的收入进行比较的时候。

justified [ˈdʒʌstifaid] *adj.* 有正当理由的，合理的

拓 justify *vt.* 证明……是正当的

justifiable *adj.* 可证明为正当的，无可非议的

同 reasonable *adj.* 合理的

例 I don't agree with those who say that sports stars' high salaries can be justified.

我不赞成有些人说体育明星高收入是合理的。

justify by 证明……是正当的（或合理的）

例 It often seems that the amount of money they are able to earn in a short time cannot possibly be justified by the amount of work they do. 他们的工作量似乎很难解释为什么在短期内能收入颇丰。

competition [ˌkɔmpiˈtiʃən] *n.* 竞争，比赛

拓 competitiveness *n.* 竞争力； competitive *adj.* 竞争的

例 So the size of salary that stars expect is closely linked to the competition they have to overcome in order to reach success. 明星对工资的期望值与他们要获得成功所必须面临的竞争有很大的联系。

peer [piə] *n.* 同等地位的人，同辈；同事

例 Modern people suffer from the peer pressure and some are not be adaptable to the competitiveness in the working position. 现代人承受着同事之间的竞争压力，有些人不能适应职场中的竞争。

veteran ['vetərən] *adj.* 经验丰富的

同 experienced *adj.* 老练的，熟练的，富有经验的

反 inexperienced *adj.* 无经验的

例 If one stays in one field for a long time, then he will become a veteran and has more chances to get promotion. 如果一个人在某个领域工作很长时间，那么他就会获得丰富的经验并有更多的晋升机会。

faculty ['fækəlti] *n.* 能力

同 capacity *n.* 能力；aptitude *n.* 天资，能力

用 have a faculty for 擅长

例 Each man is free to exercise his special faculty to the utmost. 每一个人都有尽量发挥自己特殊才能的自由。

caliber ['kælibə] *n.* 才干

用 a man of excellent caliber 才能卓越的人

例 There is no other player even remotely approaching her caliber. 就才干而言，其他选手远远赶不上她。

accumulate [ə'kju:mjuleit] *vi.* 累积

同 increase *vi.&vt.* 增加；gather *vt.* 收集
amass *vt.* 积聚，积累

用 accumulate working experience 积累工作经验

例 As they grow old, people accumulate belongings for two other reasons.
出于两个不同的原因，人们年老后喜欢收藏东西。

gender ['dʒendə] *n.* 性别

用 gender gap 性别差异

gender equality 两性平等

例 People should show respect for all employees, regardless of gender, race, religion or personality.
人们应该尊重所有的雇员，不分性别、种族、宗教信仰和个性。

思路拓展

关于工作题目中的性别平等话题。

因为现代女性接受了良好的教育（have access to good education）及技能培训（training programme），具有独立性及专业知识（independence and expertise），很多女性走进职场（women have entered the profession dominated by men in the past），事实证明她们可以与男性一样胜任工作（as capable as men）。

discrimination [dis,krimi'neiʃən] *n.* 歧视

用 gender discrimination 性别歧视

例 He has always been anti racial discrimination.
他一贯反对种族歧视。

equal ['i:kwəl] *adj.* 相等的，平等的

拓 equality *n.* 平等；inequality *n.* 不平等
equalize *vt.* 使相等
unequal *adj.* 不平等的

用 enjoy equal rights 享受平等权利
achieve equal status 实现平等地位
equal pay for equal work 同工同酬
equal employment opportunity 同等就业机会

例 The firm should distribute on the principle of equal pay for equal work.
公司应按照同工同酬的原则进行分配。

fairness ['feənis] *n.* 公平

拓 fair *adj.* 公平的；unfair *adj.* 不公平的

同 justice *n.* 正义，公道；equality *n.* 平等

例 We all know even a child can see the fairness of reasonable penalties. 我们都知道哪怕是孩子也都清楚合理处罚之公正。

promotion [prə'məuʃən] *n.* 提升，晋升

用 get promotion 升职

例 Your promotion to senior editor is now official.
现在你被正式提升为高级编辑。

mobility [məu'biliti] *n.* 流动

用 talent mobility 人才流动

例 The difference in regional house prices acts as an obstacle to mobility of labour.
不同地区房价的差异阻碍了劳动力的流动。

brain drain 人才流失

例 Brain drain is an increasingly serious problem nowadays.
如今，人才外流问题日趋严重。

reasonable ['ri:zənəbl] *adj.* 合理的，公道的

同 justifiable *adj.* 可证明为正当的，无可非议的
just *adj.* 公正的；rational *adj.* 合理的；理性的

用 reasonable payment 薪酬合理
reasonable job 适当的工作

例 Many young people are longing for a job with a more reasonable salary.
很多年轻人渴望找到一份薪酬合理的工作。

objective [əb'dʒektiv] *n.* 目标

同 goal *n.* 目标

用 career objective 职业目标

例 Many graduates become unemployed resulting from the high career objective they set. 很多毕业生未就

业的原因在于他们设定了太高的职业目标。

fruitful ['fru:tful] *adj.* 多产的；富有成效的

同 productive *adj.* 多产的；富有成效的

例 Just as Goethe says, "what we agree on makes us still and calm, while what we oppose makes our thoughts fruitful". 正如歌德所说，"我们赞同的东西使我们处之泰然，我们反对的东西才使我们的思想获得丰产。"

display [dis'plei] *vt.* 展示，展现

同 demonstrate *vt.* 证明；展示

用 display one's talent 展现才华

例 Lacking a stage to display our talent, we will switch a job to another. 如果没有可以展现才华的舞台，我们就会换工作。

give full play to 充分发挥

例 Whether one can give full play to his talents depends mostly on whether he has definite objectives or not. 一个人能否充分发挥才干，关键在于他是否有明确的目标。

pursue [pə'sju:] *vt.* 寻求，追求

同 seek *vt.&vi.* 寻求，寻找

用 pursue a green life 崇尚绿色生活方式

pursue progress 追求进步

例 Job hopping can be attributed to pursuing one's career goals.

跳槽的原因是人们为了追求自己的职业目标。

establish [is'tæbliʃ] *vt.* 确立，树立，创立（理论、声望等）

拓 establishment *n.* 确立

established *adj.* 确定的，已制定的

用 establish oneself as/in 使某人成为，使某人立足

例 Arduous work is needed to establish oneself in a field.

要想在某领域立足，就要付诸艰苦卓绝的努力。

dedication [ˌdediˈkeiʃən] *n.* 奉献，献身

同 devotion *n.* 献身，奉献，忠诚

用 one's dedication to 某人奉献于

例 His excellent skills and dedication to his work can make him successful.

他精湛的技术和对工作的执着能使他成功。

satisfaction [ˌsætisˈfækʃən] *n.* 满意，满足

拓 satisfy *vt.* 满足；*vi.* 令人满意

satisfactory *adj.* 满意的，符合要求的

satisfying *adj.* 令人满意的

例 So feelings about one's job must reflect how an individual feels about his or her life as a whole, and because of this, job satisfaction is indeed very important for the wellbeing of that person. 对工作的感受也能从整体上反映出个人对生活的感受，因此，对工作的满意度确实对一个人的幸福来说至关重要。

sense of fulfillment 成就感

例 A sense of fulfillment is also encouraged if a worker feels the job is worth doing because it contributes to the society and the economy as a whole.

如果一个人感觉自己的工作对社会和经济的发展颇具意义，随之会觉得这份工作的价值所在，那么一种成就感就会油然而生。

sense of belonging to a team 团队归属感

例 The sense of belonging to a team also produces job satisfaction because colleagues help each other to enjoy their working lives. 团队的归属感也能使员工对自己的工作有满足感，因为同事间的互助会使他们更加喜爱这份工作。

sense of responsibility 责任感

拓 sense of personal worth
个人价值观
sense of cooperation and competition
合作与竞争精神
sense of right and wrong 辨别是非
sense of obligation 责任感
sense of achievement 成就感

例 Satisfaction is also increased by a sense of responsibility for and the loyal to a team.
满足感也会随着对团队的责任感和忠诚度而提升。

suit [sjuːt] *vi.* 合适，相称

拓 suitable *adj.* 适当的，相配的

用 suit one's personal taste 适合个人品位

例 In some cases an employee is working in a job that suits neither his skills nor his personality.
有些情况下，员工从事的工作既不是其技能之所在，也不符合他的性格爱好。

option ['ɔpʃən] *n.* 选择，选择权

拓 optional *adj.* 可选择的

例 As with any career option, choosing one which best suits one's personal taste and lifestyle is crucial to securing happiness in his career. 对于职业选择而言，选择适合个人品位和生活方式的工作，对一个人在工作中获得幸福感至关重要。

interpersonal relations 人际关系

例 Some jobs are repetitive and boring, and interpersonal relations may be poor and lead to resentment.
有些工作不断地重复并令人烦闷，加之不良的同事关系，这些都可能导致员工对工作感到厌恶。

personal growth 个人发展

同 personal development 个人成长

用 seek for personal growth 寻求个人成长

例 Factors like personal growth and sense of belonging can be keys to motivating employee's performance. 个人发展和归属感这些因素对激励员工有重要作用。

pros and cons 正反两方面，利弊

同 merits and demerits 利弊

strengths and weaknesses 优缺点

advantages and disadvantages 利弊

例 When deciding whether or not to take a part-time job in college, you have to weigh the pros and cons. 当你决定是否在大学期间做兼职时，你需要权衡利弊。

get by 通过，过得去

用 get by with... 用……对付过去

例 Not everyone has to work to pay their way through school. They get by either through scholarship, family affluence or student loans. 不是所有的学生上学期间都要自己付学费。他们可以通过奖学金、家庭支持、或助学贷款解决费用问题。

tradeoff ['treid,ɔ:f] *n.* 权衡，折中

例 There is a tradeoff to be made, either you can take a job and make a little extra money, or you can have a little more free time and a little more time to study. 要做一个折中，要么做份兼职挣一些钱，要么多些自由时间和学习时间。

pursuit [pə'sju:t] *n.* 追求，寻求

例 Some students do not want to do part-time jobs perhaps because they feel their time could be better spent in other pursuits. 一些学生不愿做兼职，可能是因为他们想把时间花在想要追求的事情上。

juggle ['dʒʌgl] *vt.* 试图持稳（或接稳），力图使平衡

用 juggle a career and a family
在事业与家庭间维持一种平衡

例 Juggling a full-time job while trying to keep your grades at the highest level during college can certainly be a challenge. 在大学期间，保证学业优秀的同时又要做好全职工作，实在是一个挑战。

there is value in doing sth. 做某事有价值

反 there is no point in doing sth. 做某事没有价值

例 There is value in doing part time job to some degree but too often students just engage in mindless, risky behavior. 做兼职从一定程度上来说是有意义的，但是学生经常会陷入到一些无意识的危险之中。

switch [switʃ] *vt.&vi.* 转换

同 change *vt.* 改变；hop *vt.* 跳跃，跳过

用 switch job 换工作
switch over 转接；转做另一工作

例 A growing number of people are inclined to switch from one job to another to pursue their career objective. 越来越多的人为了追求自己的职业目标，不断地换工作。

assess [ə'ses] *vt.* 评定，估价

拓 assessment *n.* 评定，估价
assessable *adj.* 可估价的，可评价的

例 Changing jobs frequently can do one's career more harm than good. If one has been in more than three jobs over the last five years, he may need to seriously assess his job-hopping habit.

频繁地换工作对于一个人的职业生涯来说是弊大于利。如果五年之内换了三份工作，就需要认真考虑一下跳槽的习惯了。

job-hopper [jɔb'hɔpə] *n.* 跳槽者

例 Employers are often cautious about employing job-hoppers and they would want to know why they have not stayed long in any particular job. 雇主们会谨慎地考虑是否雇佣频繁跳槽的人，他们想了解应聘者为什么在任何一个工作岗位都待不长。

conservative attitude 保守态度

例 Many people hold the conservative attitude, claiming that job-hopping is not beneficial to personal development. 很多人持有保守的态度，认为跳槽对个人发展不利。

loyalty ['lɔiəlti] *n.* 忠心，忠诚

拓 loyal *adj.* 忠诚的，忠心的

例 Changing jobs frequently reflects badly on one's resilience and loyalty as an employee. 频繁地更换工作反映出员工极差的适应力和忠诚度。

initial [i'niʃəl] *adj.* 最初的

例 During the initial stage of one's career, he may find that he is not sure of which direction to take, or which job and industry will suit him best.
在职业生涯的最初阶段，可能找不到方向或是不知什么样的工作最适合自己。

directionless [di'rekʃnlɪs] *adj.* 没有方向的，没有目标的

拓 direction *n.* 方向

例 A frequent job-hopper could be seen as someone who lacks self-motivation and is directionless or prone to feeling restless at the workplace. 频繁跳槽者会被认为是在工作岗位上缺乏自我激励、毫无方向感、易于焦躁不安的人。

niche [nitʃ] *n.* 合适的职业

用 find one's own niche 找到自己合适的定位

例 Potential employers might find this acceptable and understand the need for young people to try out a few jobs before finding their "niche".
雇主认为年轻人在找到适合自己的职位之前，都要试试几份工作，这种情况是可以接受的。

grounding ['graundiŋ] *n.* 基础

同 basis *n.* 基础

例 A minimum stay of three or four years is required to give a worker good grounding.
在一个岗位至少三四年的时间，就会为日后的工作打下良好的基础。

frown upon 不悦，皱眉，不赞成

同 show disapproval 不赞成

例 However, if one is already in executive or management level, job-hopping would be frowned upon.
然而如果一个人已经在管理岗位上，就要慎重考虑跳槽了。

stressful ['stresful] *adj.* 充满压力的，紧张的

例 The economic and employment situation in many countries means that jobs are getting more, not less, stressful, requiring long hours and perhaps long journeys to work as well. 在很多国家，目前的经济和就业状况使工作变得更有压力了，主要体现在工作时间加长，上班路途也可能很远。

insecurity [ˌinsi'kjuəriti] *n.* 不安全，不牢靠，无把握

用 sense of insecurity 不安全感

例 Because of the lack of committment by employer, there is a great deal of insecurity in temporary job. 因为没有雇主的承诺，临时性的工作使人缺少安全感。

permanent ['pəːmənənt] *adj.* 永久性的，持久的，稳定的，恒定的

拓 permanence *n.* 持久，永久

同 lasting *adj.* 持久的； durable *adj.* 持久的
constant *adj.* 不变的，恒定的

反 momentary *adj.* 瞬间的，短暂的
transient *adj.* 短暂的

例 In spite of your rich experience, you always feel you are a second-class employee, sometimes even feel inferior to the permanent employees in the organization. 尽管你拥有丰富的工作经验，你也总感到自己是二等员工，有时甚至觉得自己比公司正式员工要低一等。

forego [fɔː'gəu] *vt.* 放弃

同 give up 放弃

例 Sometimes you may have to forego benefits that are exclusive for permanent staff.
有时你要放弃一些只有正式雇员才获得的利益。

链接机经关键词

工作满足感

- 因素

员工可以从很多方面获得对工作的满足感(Employees get job satisfaction in a number of ways)，几个方面的因素能促进工作的满足感(many factors contribute to job satisfaction)，主要围绕几个意识(sense)，上

级的良好反馈(positive feedback from superiors)、成就感(a sense of fulfillment)、提升自己(a sense of progress)、团队的归属感(a sense of belonging to a team or a working community)，团队的责任感和忠诚度(a sense of responsibility for and the loyal to a team)，当然如果个性和工作性质相吻合就更好了(a job that suits both their skills and their personality)。以上几个因素能促成满意感的增加(contributes to job satisfaction)。

- 公司方面

公司应该创造公平的竞争环境(create fair competition environment)、均等机会(equal opportunity)、提升机会(chance of promotion)、给员工提供自我实现的机会(self-fulfillment, self-realization)等等。

大学生找工作难

- 很多雇主不愿意招聘没有太多经验(inexperienced)的刚毕业的大学生(Many employers would not like to recruit newly graduated students without much experience.)。此外，大学生对自己的求职目标定位过高(set high career objective)，有些不切实际(unrealistic)。同时由于失业率的上升(high rate of unemployment)，导致人才的竞争愈加激烈(the competition for jobs is fierce)、且供需不平衡(the imbalance of supply and demand)使找工作雪上加霜(add insult to injury)。
- 解决之道

找工作不能纸上谈兵(be an armchair strategist)，应该有正确的职业定位(define their career goals)，不要太理想化(less idealistic)。注重专业知识和实践技能(emphasize on both academic knowledge and practical skills)，参加各类的职业培训(vocational skills training)，做到自我提升(self-lifting/self-enhancement)，增强竞争力(competitiveness)。

兼职

- 经济上独立(economically independent)，积累工作经验(accumulate working experience)，培养解决问题的能力(cultivate the ability of problem-solving)，掌握良好的沟通技巧(communicational skills)，有助于自己追求未来的职业目标(pursue their career goals)，要对自己的职业目标进行定位(define their career objective)，培养一定的竞争意识(cultivate competitive consciousness)。

跳槽

- 跳槽(switch one job to another)是个很普遍的现象(It is a common practice that…)。原因也是多方面的(manifold)：首先可能是工资问题，工资过低(unreasonable salary)会促使很多人换工作(change their jobs)；其次是环境，包括工作环境(working environment)，同事间的关系和压力(interpersonal relationship and peer pressure)，竞争环境(competitive environment)，及提升的机会(promotion)。为了寻求这些方面的平衡(strike a balance)以及实现自我价值(self-fulfillment)，很多人愿意换工作(inclined to hop from one job to another)。

性别差异

- 如今越来越多的女性走入职场(labor force)，很多女性可以充分发挥才能(give full play to talents)。男性在职场上的主导地位(men's dominance)被打破，然而性别歧视(gender discrimination)还是屡见不鲜(common occurrence)，甚至是根深蒂固 (prejudice against women is deeply rooted)，而收入不均(disparity of rewards between male and female)就是一个很突出的问题。

5. 媒体题材

考点回顾

20120707 广告的作用
20100327 看电视扼杀创造力
20090822 新闻媒体的利弊
20090516 读书与看电视
20090305 报纸的影响
20080816 媒体是否应限制犯罪细节

journalism ['dʒə:nəlizəm] *n.* 新闻业，新闻工作，新闻报道

拓 journal *n.* 日报；journalist *n.* 新闻工作者，记者

例 The culture, journalism, publishing, broadcasting, film and television undertakings developed vigorously.
文化、新闻、出版、广播和电影电视事业蓬勃发展。

coverage ['kʌvəridʒ] *n.* 新闻报道

拓 cover *vt.* 采访，报导

同 reportage *n.* 报道，新闻报道

用 coverage of the event 事件报导

例 Journalists can also add a certain prejudice or bias to their coverage of news.
记者在报导新闻时，也可能带有一定的偏见。

headline ['hedlain] *n.* 大字标题；*vt.* 大力宣传

用 headline news 头条新闻

例 Generally, when a star athlete is injured, the injury will become headline news. 一般来说，当一个明星运动员受了伤，其伤势会成为新闻头条。

barometer [bə'rɔmitə] *n.* [比喻]晴雨表，变化的标志

例 The press has the function of the barometer of the public opinion. 媒体起着舆论晴雨表的作用。

keep abreast of... 了解……的最新情况

同 keep people well-informed 使人们消息灵通

例 Many people often watch the news channel to keep abreast of the latest news.

很多人通过看新闻频道来了解最新新闻。

disseminate [di'semineit] *vt.*& *vi.* 散布，宣传，传播

同 publicize *vt.* 宣传，公布

用 disseminate information 传播信息

例 Internet and TV enable the messages to be disseminated even further.

互联网和电视可以使信息传播得更远。

omnipresent [ɔmni'prezənt] *adj.* 无所不在的，普遍存在的

同 prevalent *adj.* 流行的，普遍的

widespread *adj.* 普遍的，广泛的

pervasive *adj.* 普遍的

例 The modern media has become an omnipresent and important power in our society.

现代媒体成了社会上无所不在的一种重要力量。

code of ethics 道德准则，道德规范

例 Being honest is the important content of the professional code of ethics in journalism and the foundation of sharing information and communicating between people. 诚信是新闻职业道德规范的重要内容，同时也是人们信息沟通与交流的基础。

up-to-date [ˌʌptə'deit] *adj.* 最新的，最近的

同 up-to-the-minute *adj.* 最新的；latest *adj.* 最新的

例 Programmes specializing in pop music or TV soap operas focus more on local news, home issues and up-to-date traffic reports.
以流行音乐或肥皂剧为主的节目，会更关注当地新闻、家庭问题及最新的交通报道。

newsworthy ['nju:zwə:ði] *adj.* 有新闻价值的，值得报道的
例 It is newsworthy because it reflects a cultural attitude.
它具有新闻价值是因为它折射出了一种文化态度。

trustworthy ['trʌstˌwə:ði] *adj.* 可信赖的，可靠的
同 reliable *adj.* 可靠的，可信赖的
dependable *adj.* 可靠的，可信赖的
用 trustworthy product 可靠的产品
例 The news on TV should be trustworthy, which is the prerequisite of journalism. 电视上的新闻要值得信赖，这是新闻业的前提条件。

have a good nose 嗅觉敏锐
用 have a good nose for news 对新闻敏感，有洞察力
例 We say a good reporter must have a good nose for news.
我们说，一个好记者必须对新闻非常敏感。

objectively [əb'dʒektivli] *adv.* 客观地
拓 objectiveness *n.* 客观性
objective *adj.* 客观的，不带偏见的
例 The real function of media is to reveal the world objectively. 媒体的真正作用是客观地反映世界。

reveal [ri'vi:l] *vt.* 揭示，揭露，泄露
同 expose *vt.* 揭露，揭发；reveal；*vt.* 揭露
例 Mass media plays a crucial role in revealing public opinion, connecting the world to individuals. 大众传媒在反映舆论及沟通人与世界方面发挥着重要作用。

cover up 掩盖

用 cover up facts 掩盖事实

例 The authorities were able to cover up what really happened at the incident. 当局设法掩盖了事件的真相。

biased ['baiəst] *adj.*有偏见的；片面的

拓 bias *n.* 偏见，偏爱

同 prejudiced *adj.* 有成见的

unjust *adj.*不公平的；partial *adj.*不公平的

例 Many parents are biased against popular music.
许多父母对流行音乐有偏见。

advertising ['ædvətaiziŋ] *n.* 广告，广告业

拓 advertise *vi.* 做广告，登广告；advertisement *n.* 广告

例 The advertising industry has penetrated into every aspect in society. 广告业遍布社会生活的各个角落。

思路拓展

advertising与advertisement的区别

advertising是不可数名词，着重指广告行业；advertisement主要指发布出来的广告。

commercial [kə'məːʃəl] *n.* 商业广告

拓 commercialization *n.* 商品化，商业化

用 commercial campaign 商业活动

例 The television commercials paint an unrealistic picture of how good life is once you own their product.
电视商业广告为人们描绘了一幅不真实的画面，这个画面的内容是一旦你购买他们的产品，你的生活就会变得多么美好。

non-commercial [nɔn,kə'məːʃl] *adj.* 非商业性的

用 non-commercial purpose 非商业用途

例 Apart from promoting commercial goods, advertising

can also be used to educate and motivate the public about non-commercial issues such as AIDS, environmental reservation, family planning, etc.
除了促销商品之外，广告也有非商业用途，如引导人们了解、关注艾滋病、环境保护及计划生育等。

over-commercialisation [əuvəˌkəˌməːʃəlaiˈzeiʃən]
n. 过度商业化

例 On the other hand, there are a number of negative impacts of advertising, for example, it can create over-commercialization which can increase the frustration on people. 另一方面，广告也有负面效应，如过度的商业化会使人们不安。

consumption [kənˈsʌmpʃən] *n.* 消费；消费量

拓 consumer *n.* 消费者
consume *vt.* 消费
consuming *adj.* 消费的

同 expenditure *n.* 支出，花费

用 household consumption 家庭消费

例 People are also arguing about the increase in consumption of substances like alcohol and cigarettes after viewing the advertisements. 人们在看完烟酒的广告之后，也在讨论烟酒的消耗量增加的问题。

portray [pɔːˈtrei] *vt.* 描绘；描述

同 describe *vt.* 描述，形容； picture *vt.* 描写
depict *vt.* 描述，描画

例 Young people are likely to imitate the lifestyle portrayed in the commercials and squander money.
年轻人容易模仿广告中所描绘的生活方式而乱花钱。

tailor [ˈteilə] *vt.* 使合适

用 tailor sth. to one's popular taste 迎合大众的口味

tailor product to individual need
使产品符合个性需求

例 If it is true, then, that newspapers and TV stations are tailoring their news to their readers' and viewers' requirements, how can they possibly be reporting real events in an honest and objective light?
如果这是真实的，那么报纸和电视就会使它们的新闻迎合大众的口味，那还怎么可能以真实和客观的角度报道事件呢？

competition [ˌkɔmpiˈtiʃən] *n.* 竞争，角逐

拓 competitive *adj.* 竞争的
competitiveness *n.* 竞争力
competitor *n.* 竞争者

例 Advertising can also increase competition and it can create advertisement war within competitors.
广告能促进竞争，从而使竞争对手打起广告战。

positioning [pəˈziʃəniŋ] *n.* 定位

用 product positioning 产品定位

例 Moreover, it can increase the brand positioning in the market and make the brand visible.
此外，这样能够巩固产品在市场的定位，使该品牌受到公众关注。

bombard [bɔmˈbɑːd] *vt.*（用问题、建议等）不断攻击，向……连续提出问题

用 be bombarded with 充斥着……

例 People are bombarded by violence and crimes on TV.
电视节目中不断出现暴力和犯罪的画面。

sway [swei] *vt.* 使摇动；影响；*vi.* 摇摆；影响；*n.* 摇摆，摇动

同 affect *vt.* 影响

用 be swayed by 在……影响下
under the sway of 在……支配之下；在……影响下

例 It is fairly difficult to say that people will be swayed by the advertising.
很难说人们是否会受到广告的影响。

follow...blindly 盲从

用 follow the fashion blindly 盲目追逐时尚

例 People should be rational consumers and avoid being misled by false information on the commercials to follow the trend blindly.
人们应该做理性的消费者，避免被商业广告中的虚假信息误导而盲目跟风。

squander ['skwɔndə] *vt.&vi.* 浪费

用 squander time in doing sth. 浪费时间做某事
squander money 浪费金钱

例 He squandered too much time watching TV.
他把大量的时间都浪费在了看电视上。

impulsively [im'pʌlsivli] *adv.* 冲动地，易冲动地

拓 impulsive *adj.* 冲动的；impulsiveness *n.* 冲动

例 Consumers may not actually need the products but they buy them impulsively soon after they watch the advertisements. 消费者可能并不需要这些产品，但是他们在看完广告后就冲动地购买了。

propaganda [ˌprɔpə'gændə] *n.* 宣传，鼓吹

拓 propagandise *vt.* 宣传；*vi.* 进行宣传
propagandism *n.* 宣传

同 agitprop *n.* 宣传鼓动；publicity *n.* 宣传

用 make propaganda for... 为……宣传

例 The government produced much political propaganda.
政府进行了大量的政治宣传。

fake [feik] *adj.* 欺骗的，假的；伪造的

同 false *adj.* 伪造的；counterfeit *adj.* 假冒的，伪造的
fraudulent *adj.* 欺骗性的

用 fake advertising 虚假广告
fake commodities 假冒商品

例 Fake advertisement draws more and more attentions and becomes a serious social problem. 虚假广告吸引了越来越多的关注，成为一个严重的社会问题。

fraudulent ['frɔːdjulənt] *adj.* 欺骗性的，不诚实的

拓 fraud *n.* 欺骗； fraudulence *n.* 欺诈，欺骗性
fraudulency *n.* 欺诈，诈骗

同 deceptive *adj.* 欺诈的； treacherous *adj.* 奸诈的
fallacious *adj.* 谬误的，骗人的；fake *adj.* 伪造的

例 Some information on the Internet is misleading and fraudulent. 网上的一些信息具有误导性和欺骗性。

trick [trik] *vt.&vi.* 欺骗，哄骗；*n.* 诡计，计谋

同 cheat *vt.&vi.* 欺骗；deceive *vt.&vi.* 欺骗
fool *vt.&vi.* 欺骗

用 be tricked by 被……所欺骗
be at one's trick 捉弄人
play (put) a trick on someone 欺骗某人
tricks of the trade 某一门职业或生意的诀窍
dirty tricks 卑鄙的手段

例 Without the strict censorship, people are constantly tricked by advertisements on TV. 没有严格的审查制度，人们会时常被电视中的广告所欺骗。

uncensored [ʌn'sensəd] *adj.* （出版物）未经审查的；（言论等）无约束的

拓 censor *vt.* 审查；censorship *n.* 审查制度

用 uncensored news reports 未受审查的新闻报道

例 In a sense, some uncensored information is likely to corrupt children's minds. 从一定意义上来说，一些未经审查的信息可能会腐蚀孩子的心灵。

exaggeration [igˌzædʒəˈreiʃən] *n.* 夸张，夸大之词

拓 exaggerate *vi.* 夸大，夸张

exaggerated *adj.* 夸张的，言过其实的

同 overstatement *n.* 大话，夸大的叙述

例 People buy the products impulsively due to the exaggeration of the advertisements. 由于广告的夸大宣传，人们冲动地购买了某些产品。

over-emphasize [ˌəuvəˈemfəsaiz] *vt.&vi.*（使）过分强调

例 Advertising usually over-emphasizes the features of the products or the services.

广告通常会过分地渲染产品或服务的特色。

intrude [inˈtruːd] *vi.* 侵入，打扰

拓 intrusion *n.* 侵入，打扰

intrusive *adj.* 侵入的，打扰的

同 encroach *vt.* 侵犯；trespass *vi.* 打扰；冒犯

用 intrude on (infringe on) someone's privacy 侵犯隐私

例 Some paparazzi often intrude on stars' privacy so as to get the sensational news. 狗仔队为了获得引起轰动的新闻，经常侵犯明星们的隐私。

nuisance [ˈnjuːsəns] *n.* 讨厌的人（或事）；恼人之事

用 make oneself a nuisance 被人讨厌

例 Excessive advertising has become a nuisance in most cities of the world.

在大多数的城市中，过多的广告很令人讨厌。

expectancy [ikˈspektənsi] *n.* 期望，期待

拓 expect *vt.* 期望；*vi.* 期待

同 expectation *n.* 期待，预期；prospect *n.* 预期

用 expectancy of value 预期值

例 If young people like alcohol ads, they are more likely to have positive expectancies about alcohol use and to intend to drink.

如果年轻人喜欢酒类广告，他们就很有可能对饮酒抱有很高的期望，也就很可能喝酒。

perception [pə'sepʃən] *n.* 感觉；观念；洞察力

例 Exposure to alcohol advertising shapes attitudes and perceptions about alcohol use among young people.

酒类广告能够塑造青少年对饮酒的态度和观念。

ramification [ˌræmifi'keiʃən] *n.* 结果，后果

例 The consequences and ramifications of the mass media relate not merely to the way newsworthy events are perceived, but also to a multitude of cultural influences that operate through the media.

大众传媒不但对人们如何看待那些具有新闻价值的事件产生影响，同时也产生大量的文化影响。

subliminal [səb'liminəl] *adj.* 潜意识的，下意识的

拓 subliminally *adv.* 下意识地，潜意识地

同 sub-conscious *adj.* 下意识的

例 Subliminal advertising in magazines is based on the fact that under any circumstances, you store more information in a fraction of a second and are influenced by it—than you are ever consciously aware of.

杂志上的潜意识广告会让你在任何情况下瞬间记住信息，在潜意识中就受其影响了。

obesity [əu'bisiti] *n.* 过度肥胖

拓 obese *adj.* 肥胖的，过胖的

例 There are millions of adolescents fighting against obesity, but at the same time they are exposed to

thousands of advertisements of junk food.
成千上万的青少年都在努力减肥，但与此同时他们会接触到大量的垃圾食品广告。

exclusively [ik'sklu:sivli] *adv.* 专有地，排外地；唯一地

拓 exclusive *adj.* 独有的；*n.* 独家新闻

例 Some advertisements including food, toys, music and clothes are designed exclusively to target children.
有些广告如食品广告、玩具广告、音乐广告及服装广告都是专门针对于儿童的。

glue [glu:] *vt.* 似用胶固定，使不移动

用 glue one's eyes to… 目不转睛地看……

例 Parents don't like to see their children gluing their eyes to the TV for hours. 父母们不愿看到自己的孩子连续几个小时目不转睛地看电视。

excessive [ik'sesiv] *adj.* 过度的，过多的

拓 excessively *adv.* 过分地
excessiveness *n.* 过度，冗余

用 excessive violent and pornographic contents
过多的暴力与色情内容

例 Those kids have been linked to excessive use of violent video games and war images.
孩子们接触了过多的暴力游戏和战争场面。

pornography [pɔ:'nɔgrəfi] *n.* 色情；黄色电影

拓 pornographic *adj.* 色情的

同 obscene *adj.* 淫秽的

例 We ought to strengthen our supervision over the TV programmes which the children watch, leaving them no chances to be exposed to violence and pornography.
我们应该加强对儿童所观看的电视节目的监管，不让他们有机会接触充满暴力和色情的节目。

misguide [mis'gaid] *vt.* 误导，使误入歧途

拓 misguided *adj.* 被误导的；misguiding *adj.* 误导人的

同 mislead *vt.* 误导

用 misguide teenagers 误导青少年

例 Some exaggerated advertisements misguide consumers without mentioning the side effects of the products.
有些广告夸大宣传，不提及产品的副作用，误导消费者。

entertainment [ˌentə'teinmənt] *n.* 娱乐，消遣

拓 entertaining *adj.* 令人愉快的，使人得到娱乐的
entertain *vt.* 娱乐

用 to the entertainment of 使感到有趣的是……

例 Television is not only a convenient source of entertainment, but also a comparatively cheap one.
电视不仅是一种便于获得娱乐的方式，同时也是一种相对便宜的娱乐方式。

isolated ['aisəleitid] *adj.* 孤立的

拓 isolate *vt.* 使隔离，使孤立；isolation *n.* 隔离，孤立

例 Watching too much TV, people , especially youngsters, may become violent, isolated, aggressive and eccentric. 人们（尤其是年轻人）看太多电视会变得暴力、孤僻、有攻击性及古怪。

couch potato 老坐在电视机前的人，终日懒散的人

例 They intended to do some exercise today but ended up being a couch potato and watching TV all day.
他们今天本来要做一些运动，结果却躺在沙发上看了一整天的电视。

背景知识

随着电视业的发展，出现了一类喜欢把大把时间用在看电视上的人，我们通常将这类人称为“电视

迷”，英文的表达方式就是couch potato。couch指坐卧两用的长沙发，potato指土豆，couch potato就是指那些一有时间就坐在沙发上看电视的人。

exposure [iks'pəuʒə] *n.* 显露，暴露

例 However a negative influence in teenagers is the use of cigars by movie stars, the excessive images of violence and exposure to thousands of junk food advertisements. 然而对青少年的负面影响在于孩子们看到电影明星抽雪茄，过多的暴力场景及众多的垃圾食品广告。

violence ['vaiələns] *n.* 激烈；暴力

拓 violent *adj.* 暴力的；猛烈的

例 Of all the media distribution channels the most influential one has been the television, for we are constantly exposed to thousands of images of violence and advertising。电视是所有媒体形式中最具影响力的一种，我们从中不断接触到很多的暴力场面和广告。

aggressive [ə'gresiv] *adj.* 好斗的，侵略性的

拓 aggressively *adv.* 侵略地；攻击地

aggressiveness *n.* 攻击性；侵犯

例 Critics of television violence say that when children watch an endless stream of violent acts, they become desensitised to the damaging effects of aggressive behaviour and feel less sympathy for the victims of aggressive acts. 电视暴力的批评家们认为孩子经常看电视上的暴力场景，就会对攻击性的行为带来的后果变得麻木，对受害者缺乏同情心。

desensitise [ˌdiː'sensitaiz] *vt.* 使不敏感，使麻木不仁

用 desensitise to… 对……麻木

例 Seeing too much violence on television can desensitise people to it.

人们在电视上看到太多的暴力就会对之麻木。

immune [i'mju:n] *adj.* 免疫的，不受影响的

用 be immune to 不受……影响

例 We have become immune to bad news and the newspapers and radio stations are aware of this.
我们对坏消息变得麻木了，报业和电台也意识到了这一点。

numb [nʌm] *vt.* 使麻木；*adj.* 冷淡的，无感情的

拓 numbness *n.* 麻木，麻痹

用 become numb to… 对……麻木

例 People's numb attitude towards violence is scary.
人们对暴力的麻木让人感觉恐怖。

reality and fantasy 现实与虚幻

用 distinguish between reality and fantasy
分辨现实与虚幻

例 Television presents many unwholesome attitudes about sexuality, violence, and ethics that may psychologically influence people who have less discernment between reality and fantasy. 电视上有太多关于性、暴力和伦理方面的内容，从心理上影响着那些还不能正确看待现实与虚幻的人们。

immobilise [i'məubilaiz] *vt.* 使不动，使固定

拓 mobile *adj.* 机动的；易变的
mobilise *vt.* 动员，调动；immobilisation *n.* 固定

例 We may decide to catch a one-hour programme, but find ourselves immobilised by TV's power and end up watching longer than we originally planned.
我们可能打算看一个小时的节目，结果却在电视机前一动不动，到头来看的时间比预计的长得多。

ensnare [in'sneə] *vt.* 使（落）入圈套；勾引

用 be ensnared by… 受迷惑

例 Once we start watching, it is all too easy to become ensnared in its almost hypnotic power to keep us watching regardless of the banality of the content.
一旦我们看上电视，就很容易陷入电视的魔力之中，不管节目多么无聊，也会一直不停地看。

regulate ['regjuleit] *vt.* 管理，控制

拓 regulation *n.* 管理

同 govern *vt.* 管理；control *vt.* 控制，管理
manage *vt.* 管理

例 Advertising needs to be strictly regulated and restricted.
我们应该对广告业进行严格的监管和限制。

restrict [ris'trikt] *vt.* 限制，限定，约束

拓 restriction *n.* 限制，约束

同 restrain *vt.* 约束；confine *vt.* 限制

用 be restricted to 仅限于……，局限于……
be restricted within 限于……

例 Some people assert that restricting the amount of violence in media can lessen violent crimes in society.
有些人认为限制媒体上的暴力情节可以减少社会中的暴力犯罪。

censorship ['sensəʃip] *n.* 审查，检查；审查制度

拓 censor *vt.* 审查；uncensored *adj.* 未经审查的

用 censorship of the press 新闻审查制度
relax censorship 放宽审查

例 Government should establish and impose a strict censorship on all mass media.
政府应该建立和实施针对所有媒体的严格的审查制度。

supervision [ˌsjuːpəˈviʒən] *n.* 监督，管理

拓 supervise *vt.*& *vi.* 监督，管理

supervisor *n.* 监察人，管理者

同 regulation *n.* 管理

例 Proper supervision and guidance in the advertising is highly necessary. 广告业急需恰当的监管与引导。

链接机经关键词

媒体的特点

- 信息性

  媒体是当今最流行和最广泛的信息平台。通过媒体人们可迅速地获取最新的消息(the latest news)，与时俱进(keep up with the times)。

- 娱乐性

  媒体具有很强的娱乐性(entertaining)，能让人放松(enable people to relax)，并能丰富人们的生活(enrich people's life)。

- 教育性

  媒体具有教育的功能(play the educational role)，能够传播知识(spread knowledge)，开拓人们的眼界(broaden people's horizon)。

媒体的负面作用

- 信息爆炸(information overload/explosion)有时使我们无法选择信息，因为太过浪费时间(squander time)。
- 媒体中的植入广告(built-in advertisements)和潜意识广告(subliminal advertisements)令人十分烦扰(nuisance)。媒体有时会传播虚假广告(fake/false advertising)。
- 缺少严厉的监管(supervision)及审查制度(censorship)，暴力(violence)和色情(pornography)内容

没有得到严格的控制。未经审查的信息极易腐蚀小孩的心灵(uncensored information corrupts children's minds)。

- 网络犯罪(cyber crime)，是目前犯罪的一个新渠道(new channel)。

记者应具备的素质

- 新闻记者报道新闻(report news)要全面(show the whole picture/whole story)，要保证公正(remain impartial)，不能隐瞒真相(The truth cannot be suppressed.)，也不能大肆渲染(while others are highlighted)。
- 新闻记者报道新闻要客观(objective)，不能随意加入主观的喜好(preferences)。新闻报道的职责是报道事实(report the truth)，而不应该片面刻意地追求轰动效应(sensational effect)，也不能屈服于各方面的压力(bow to the pressure)，这样才能报道出值得信赖的(trustworthy)和具有新闻价值(newsworthy)的新闻。

6. 国际化与发展题材

考点回顾

20100626	国际旅游带来偏见还是开阔视野
20100109	慈善组织帮助最需要的人
20090207	国际援助
20081120	国际旅游
20080726	国际合作的好处

tourism ['tuərizəm] *n.* 旅游，旅游业

拓 tour *n.* 旅游，旅行；tourist *n.* 旅行者

用 tourism activities 旅游活动

tourism industry 旅游业

tourism marketing 旅游营销

tourism resource 旅游资源

例 It may seem that tourism brings only benefits, but further consideration shows that it also has disadvantages. 看似旅游业带来的只有好处，但你仔细考虑就会发现它也具有弊端。

recreation [ˌrekri'eiʃn] *n.* 娱乐，消遣

拓 recreational *adj.* 娱乐的，消遣的

同 amusement *n.* 消遣，娱乐

entertainment *n.* 消遣，娱乐

relaxation *n.* 消遣，娱乐，放松

例 Tourism is the act of travel for the purpose of not only recreation, but also the process of experiencing. 旅游不仅是为了休闲放松，也是一种体验的过程。

catering ['keitəriŋ] *n.* 饮食服务；包办食品

用 catering business 饮食业；catering service 饮食服务

例 It might occupy local services such as entertainment, accommodation and catering for tourists.
它会为游客提供娱乐、住宿及餐饮服务。

cuisine [kwi'zi:n] *n.* 烹饪，菜肴

例 The increased exposure to the local culture, local cuisine, local economy, and environment inherently leads to enriching experiences. 多接触当地的文化、美食、经济和环境会丰富人生体验。

taxation [tæk'seiʃən] *n.* 税收，纳税

同 revenue *n.* 税收

例 Many countries depend heavily upon travel expenditures by foreigners as a source of taxation and as a source of income for the local people.
很多国家依赖于外国游客带来的税收，把它当做当地人收入的来源。

export [eks'pɔ:t] *vi.&vt.* 出口，输出；*n.* 输出，出口

拓 exportable *adj.* 可出口的，可输出的

反 import *vt.* 输入，进口

用 gross export 出口总额

例 Therefore, the development of tourism is often a strategy to promote a particular region for the purpose of increasing commerce through exporting goods and services. 因此，发展旅游业通常是带动地区发展的一种策略——通过产品和服务输出促进贸易发展。

occupation [ˌɔkju'peiʃən] *n.* 职业

用 blind alley occupation 没有前途的职业

例 Tourism provides direct employment for the people associated with occupations in bars and hotels. 旅游业能够带动相关行业的就业，如酒吧和旅馆。

infrastructure ['infrəˌstrʌktʃə] *n.* 基础设施，公共建设

用 infrastructure construction 基础设施建设

例 Wildlife can be adversely affected by the construction and maintenance of tourist infrastructure, and by tourist activities. 基础设施的建设与维护以及游客的参观活动会给野生动物带来负面的影响。

artificial [ˌɑ:ti'fiʃəl] *adj.* 人造的，人工的；人为的

用 artificial intelligence 人工智能
artificial satellite 人造卫星

例 In addition, in order to attract tourists, a lot of artificial facilities have been built, which have certain

unfavourable effects on the environment here.
另外，为了吸引游客，这里修建了大量设施，对环境产生了不利的影响。

graffiti [grə'fiːtiː] *n.* 墙上乱写乱画的东西（graffito的复数形式）；*vt.* 在……上涂鸦，涂写

例 The ultimate goal is to leave a very selective record of one's visit: no traces at camp sites; zero pollution of air and water; properly disposed of waste; no graffiti pollution and fair compensation for resources used.
最终的目标是要留下该留下的足迹，而不要在露营的地方留下痕迹，不要污染空气和水，要恰当地处理废物，不要涂鸦，对于使用的资源要有合理的补偿。

vandalism ['vændəlizəm] *n.* 故意破坏文物的行为

例 Tourism undermines culture by commercialising it and this is often connected with increasing litter, graffiti, vandalism and noise, tourists do not always respect traditional cultures, which is sad but true.
旅游业的商业化破坏了文化，这种破坏通常表现为随处乱扔垃圾、随意涂鸦、故意破坏文物、制造噪音等，游客总是不能尊重当地的传统文化，这一点实在令人遗憾但却是事实。

ecotourism [ˌiːkəu'tuərizəm] *n.* 生态旅游，生态旅行

例 Ecotourism can be more prosperous as a green industry, which aspires to give indigenous people an opportunity to realise fair income and to raise them up from poverty.
生态旅游作为绿色产业前景远大。生态旅游能够令本土居民获得可观的收入，摆脱贫困。

ecosystem ['i:kəusistəm] *n.* 生态系统

用 agricultural ecosystem 农业生态系统

例 Increasing tourists are visiting areas where the ecosystem is fragile and resources are scarce. 越来越多的游客涌入到生态系统脆弱、资源匮乏的地区。

sensitive ['sensitiv] *adj.* 敏感的

例 The travellers must reexamine their behaviour and become more sensitive to their impact on the local environment, both natural and cultural.
游客必须要重新认识自己的行为，意识到其对当地的自然环境和人文环境造成的影响。

conscientious [,kɔnʃi'enʃəs] *adj.* 按良心办事的；认真的；尽责的

拓 conscientiously *adv.* 良心上
conscientiousness *n.* 尽责；凭良心办事

例 In such cases, as a conscientious government, we have to know what is right for the local people.
在这样的情况下，作为一个对人民负责的政府，我们必须了解对当地人来说什么是对的。

indigenous [in'didʒinəs] *adj.* 本土的，国产的；固有的；土著的

用 indigenous population 土著

例 The traveller must learn the cultural and social taboos and the local customs and tradition, choose accommodations which maintain cultural identity by using forms of indigenous architecture.
游客应了解当地的一些文化和社会的禁忌、风俗和传统，选择能展现文化特征的本土建筑住宿。

aboriginal [æbə'ridʒənl] *adj.* 土著的；原始的；*n.* 土著居民

拓 aboriginally *adv.* 从最初，原来

aboriginality *n.* 本土性；原始状态

用 aboriginal inhabitants 土著居民

例 The over-exploitation of the natural resources forced the aboriginals out of their home.
自然资源的过度开发，迫使很多土著居民背井离乡。

conflict ['kɔnflikt] *n.* 冲突，矛盾

拓 conflicting *adj.* 相矛盾的，不一致的

同 contradiction *n.* 矛盾

用 cultural conflict 文化冲突

例 You will experience much tension in cultural conflict.
你将会经历许多文化冲突带来的压力。

heritage ['heritidʒ] *n.* 遗产；传统

用 heritage preservation 遗产保护

例 The ancient buildings are a part a of the national heritage.
这些古建筑是民族遗产的一部分。

mutual ['mju:tʃuəl] *adj.* 相互的，彼此的

拓 mutually *adv.* 互相地

用 mutual aid 互助
mutual exclusion 互斥现象，互斥
mutual trust 相互信任
mutual understanding 相互理解

例 If the international tourism is encouraged, mutual understanding between different peoples will be enhanced. 如果国际旅游得到鼓励推进，那么不同国家人民的相互了解就能得到增进。

tension ['tenʃən] *n.* 紧张；*vt.* 使紧张

同 tenseness *n.* 紧张；stress *n.* 紧张；tensity *n.* 紧张

例 Many people tend to support that the international travel can lessen the tension between different countries.
很多人认为国际旅游可以缓解国家间的紧张局势。

distinct [dis'tiŋkt] *adj.* 清楚的；明显的；独特的

拓 distinctly *adv.* 明显地；distinction *n.* 区别，差别
distinctive *adj.* 有特色的，与众不同的
distinctively *adv.* 特殊地，区别地

用 distinct from 与……不同

例 For lack of distinct culture, some places will not attract tourists any more.
由于缺乏独特的文化，有些地方不再吸引游客。

exotic [ig'zɔtik] *adj.* 异国的；异国情调的；奇异的

拓 exoticism *n.* 异国情调，异国风味

例 When you travel abroad the customs and culture can seem very exotic. 当你出国旅行，必能感受到奇异的风俗习惯与文化。

natural landscape 自然景观

例 Many people today enjoy the pleasure of travelling around the world and appreciating exotic cultures and natural landscapes. 现在很多人都热爱环球旅行，可以感受异国文化，欣赏自然风光。

driving force 推动力；促进

同 impetus *n.* 推动力；促进

例 Travel has become a lifestyle for some people, and has turned out to be the driving force in GDP growth for some countries. 旅游对很多人来说已经成为一种生活方式，也成为一些国家提高国内生产总值的推动力。

captivate ['kæptiveit] *vt.* 迷住，迷惑

同 fascinate *vt.* 使着迷；attract *vt.&vi.*. 吸引

例 The allure and charm of Paris captivate all that visit there.
巴黎的诱惑与魅力令所有到此游玩的人着迷。

diversity [dai'və:siti] *n.* 多样性，差异

拓 diverse *adj.* 变化多的，多种多样的

diversify *vt.* 使多样化

用 maintain cultural diversity 保持文化的多样性

例 Cultural diversity is as important as bio-diversity, yet it is probably more endangered and less protected.
文化多样性就像生物多样性一样重要，但其受到了威胁，没有得到有效的保护。

identity [ai'dentiti] *n.* 身份；同一性，一致

用 national identity 国家认同
cultural identity 文化认同

例 Some people say that the increasing business and cultural contact between countries is a positive development, while others think that many countries will lose their national identities. 一些人认为加强国家间的贸易和文化往来是一种积极的发展，而另外一些人认为很多国家会从中丢失他们国家的特性。

boundary ['baundəri] *n.* 分界线；边界，范围

同 bound *n.* 范围；border *n.* 边界

用 without boundary 没有边界

例 Due to globalisation, the business market in the world has no boundaries.
由于全球化，商业变得无国界。

multilateral [ˌmʌlti'lætərəl] *adj.* 多边的；多方面的

用 multilateral agreement 多边合约
multilateral trade 多边贸易

例 The UN is the centre of international multilateral mechanisms and the key platform for making multilateralism work. 联合国是国际多边机制的核心，是实践多边主义的重要舞台。

showcase ['ʃəukeis] *vt.* 使展现；*n.* 展示

例 Hosting the Olympics and the Paralympics is a source

of national pride for China and a way to showcase the country on the international stage. 主办奥运会和残奥会是中国增强人民国家荣誉感的源泉之一，也是中国在世界的舞台上展示自己实力的机会。

pitfall ['pitfɔːl] *n.* 缺陷；陷阱，圈套

同 snare *n.* 陷阱，圈套； trap *n.* 陷阱，圈套

例 Globalisation has got tremendous benefits as well as its own pitfalls. 全球化好坏参半。

integration [ˌinti'greiʃn] *n.* 结合；综合；一体化

拓 integrate *vt.* 使……完整

integrated *adj.* 综合的，完整的

例 Globalisation means increasing the interdependence, connectivity and integration on a global level with respect to the social, cultural, political, technological, economic and ecological levels. 全球化意味着世界各国在社会、文化、政治、科技、经济和生态环保方面相互依赖、联系及融合。

misapprehension [misæpri'henʃ(ə)n] *n.* 误解，误会

拓 misapprehend *vt.* 误会，误解

misapprehensive *adj.* 误会的，误解的

同 misunderstanding *n.* 误解，误会

例 World Expo can build up a bridge for people all over the world to clear up misapprehension, improve mutual understanding and balance oppositions.

世博会可以为各国人民消除误解、增进相互了解、化解矛盾架起一座沟通的桥梁。

estrangement [is'treindʒmənt] *n.* 疏远

拓 estrange *vt.* 使疏远，离间

estranged *adj.* 不和的，疏远的

例 People should do away with hostility, estrangement and

prejudice, respecting and tolerating other cultures with an open mind. 人们应该以一种开放的心态来尊重和包容异国文化，消除对别国的敌意、疏远和偏见。

standard of living（亦作 living standard）生活水平，生活标准

例 Proponents of globalisation argue that it allows poor countries and their citizens to develop economically and raise their standards of living. 支持者认为全球化能够帮助贫困国家及其人民发展经济，提高生活水平。

cultural hegemony 文化霸权

例 We should enhance national cohesion and solidarity while fighting against the intrusion of cultural hegemony. 我们应该增强民族的凝聚力和向心力，同时抵制文化霸权主义的侵袭。

infiltrate ['infiltreit] *vt.&vi.*（使）渗透

拓 infiltration *n.* 渗透

infiltrated *adj.* 渗透的，浸润的

用 infiltrate through 渗透

例 Many wrong thoughts and values may infiltrate into people's minds. 很多错误的想法和价值观会渗透进人们的心里。

gap between the rich and poor 贫富差距

例 Giving aid to poorer countries may help them shake off the poverty and narrow the gap between the rich and poor. 援助贫困国家可以帮助他们摆脱贫困，缩小贫富差距。

写作提示

imbalance与gap/disparity

相关的雅思作文话题：城乡发展不平衡、穷富差距、发展与环境保护不平衡、男女地位不平衡、传统

观念与现代观念（代沟）。已成为社会中的（hot-button issue）敏感问题。贫富差距的不断扩大会激起人们的仇富心理（resentment against the rich）。

disparity [dis'pæriti] *n.* 不等，不同；不一致

同 difference *n.* 差异，不同
disagreement *n.* 不一致
discrepancy *n.* 不一致

用 disparity between the rich and poor 贫富差距
narrow the urban-rural disparity 缩小城乡差距

例 Income disparity between urban and rural residents is a big issue affecting one country's economic development and social stability.
城乡居民收入差距问题是关系到一个国家经济发展和社会稳定的大问题。

bridge [bridʒ] *vt.* 把……弥合（或连接）起来

用 bridge the gap between the rich and poor
缩小贫富差距

例 These tax reforms attempt to bridge the gap between the rich and poor.
这些税收改革旨在弥合贫富之间的差距。

donor ['dəunə] *n.* 捐赠者，赠送人

拓 donation *n.* 捐赠；捐款，捐赠物

同 contributor *n.* 贡献者，捐助者

用 donor country (donating country) 援助国

例 Aid is primarily designed to serve the strategic and economic interests of the donor countries. 援助的最主要目的是为了捐助国的战略和经济利益。

philanthropic [filən'θrɔpik] *adj.* 博爱的；慈善的

拓 philanthropist *n.* 慈善家，乐善好施的人

philanthropism *n.* 博爱，博爱主义

同 charitable *adj.* 慷慨的；仁慈的；慈善事业的

benevolent *adj.* 慈善的，仁慈的

humanitarian *adj.* 人道主义的，博爱的

例 There are remarkable experiences and outstanding achievements in the field of the philanthropic donation abroad. 国外的慈善业已积累了丰富的经验并做出了非凡的贡献。

humanitarian [hju'mæni,teəriən] *adj.* 人道主义的；博爱的；*n.* 人道主义者

拓 humanitarianism *n.* 人道主义

同 merciful *adj.* 仁慈的，慈悲的，宽容的

philanthropic *adj.* 博爱的；慈善的

benevolent *adj.* 慈善的，仁慈的

用 humanitarian aid 人道主义援助

例 It seems that aids should be given to poorer countries for humanitarian reasons. But some advanced countries donate money for economical, political or diplomatic reasons. 援助贫困国家应该是出于人道主义，但是很多发达国家的捐助是出于经济、政治或外交方面的原因。

beneficence [bi'nefisəns] *n.* 善行；仁慈；赠物

拓 beneficent *adj.* 慈善的，善行的

同 kindness *n.* 仁慈，好意

例 There exists a potential danger of the abuse of the beneficence by some corrupt governmental officials and inefficient administration. 由于存在着腐败的政府官员和无能的管理，援助物资有被滥用的潜在危险。

assistance [ə'sistəns] *n.* 援助，帮助

拓 assist *vt.* 帮助； assistant *adj.* 辅助的，有帮助的

同 help *n.* 帮助；aid *n.* 帮助，援助

用 international assistance 国际援助

例 Financial and technical assistance should be aimed exclusively at promoting the economic and social progress of developing countries and should not in any way be used by the developed countries to the detriment of the national sovereignty of recipient countries.
经济和科技的援助应缘于促进发展中国家的经济和社会进步，而决不能是发达国家对援助国家的主权上的侵害。

obligation [ˌɔbli'geiʃən] *n.* 义务，职责

用 fail one's obligation 没能履行承诺

例 Even though these targets and agendas have been set, year after year almost all rich nations have constantly failed to reach their agreed obligations.
尽管可能设定了目标及议程，但年复一年，几乎所有的富国都没能履行其约定的职责。

moral ['mɔːrəl] *adj.* 道德的，精神上的；道义上的

拓 morally *adv.* 道德上，有道德地

例 People around the world have a moral obligation to help each other.
世界上的人们在道义上都有互相帮助的责任。

make sense 有意义，合乎情理

用 make economic sense 有经济意义
make moral sense 道义上的意义

例 Increasing aid and market access for poor countries makes sense. 对穷国增加援助并使其进入市场有一定的意义。

relieve [ri'liːv] *vt.* 解除，减轻；救济，援救

同 alleviate *vt.* 减轻，缓和；lighten *vt.* 减轻

assuage *vt.* 缓和，减轻；mitigate *vt.* 使缓和，使减轻

用 relieve the pressure 缓和压力

relieve from... 从……中解除

relieve stress 减压，缓解压力

relieve the sufferings 减少痛苦

relieve one's feelings 发泄感情，泄愤

relieve oneself 使自己放松；大小便

例 They are trying to build up funds to relieve the poverty-stricken families.

他们设法筹集资金来救济非常贫困的家庭。

get rid of 摆脱，除去

同 remove *vt.&vi.* 移走；排除

exterminate *vt.* 消灭，根除

eliminate *vt.* 消除，排除； uproot *vt.* 根除

用 get rid of poverty 摆脱贫困

例 Mutual assistance enhances friendship between countries, which helps get rid of the possibility of wars due to misunderstanding. 相互援助有助于提高国家间的友谊，消除国家间由于误解导致战争的可能性。

shake off 摆脱，丢弃

同 shirk off 逃避

用 shake off poverty 摆脱贫困，脱贫

shake off backwardness 摆脱落后

shake off the duty 推卸责任

例 Generally speaking, their lives are better than before, and the government and society are helping them shake off poverty. 总的来说，他们的生活也比过去好一些了，国家和社会正在帮助他们摆脱贫困。

poverty-stricken ['pɔvətiˌstrikən] *adj.* 极度贫困的，贫穷的

同 needy countries 贫困国家

impoverished countries 贫困国家

underdeveloped countries 贫困国家

例 Aid from rich countries is just a disguised way to exploit cheap natural resources and get great benefits from poverty-stricken countries.

富国只是用这种手段掩盖自己从贫困国家掠夺廉价自然资源并从中受益的事实。

needy ['ni:di] *adj.* 贫穷的，贫困的，生活艰苦的

同 underprivileged *adj.* 贫困的；社会地位低下的

indigent *adj.* 贫困的

用 the needy people 贫困人民；needy country 贫困国家

例 The aid from developed countries is of great benefit to common people in needy countries. 发达国家的援助给贫困国家的人们带来巨大的益处。

medical care 医疗护理

用 improvement of medical care system

改进医疗保健体系

例 The aid from rich countries provides good medical care and helps promote the development of education, agriculture and economy.

富裕国家可以提供良好的医疗援助，促进教育、农业及经济的发展。

cut back 修剪；削减

同 cut down 减少

用 cut back on spending 削减经费

例 In the context of international obligations, it is criticised by many as an excuse for rich countries to cut back aid that has been agreed and promised. 在国际环境的背景下，富国如果找借口减少所承诺的援助，会遭到谴责。

long-term [ˈlɔŋtəːm] *adj.* 长期的

用 long-term cooperation 长期合作

long-term loan 长期贷款

例 Developed countries will provide, to the greatest extent possible, an increased flow of aid for developing countries on a long-term and continuing basis. 发达国家应该尽可能对发展中国家提供长期的和持续的援助。

misspend [ˌmisˈspend] *vt.* 滥用；乱花，浪费

同 misuse *vt.* 误用；滥用

用 misspend time 虚度时光；misspend youth 浪费青春

例 Many people think that countries have a moral obligation to help each other, while others argue that the aid money is misspent by the governments that receive it. 很多人认为国家之间出于人道主义应该相互援助，而其他人认为受援助的政府会滥用援助资金。

abuse [əˈbjuːs] *n.* 滥用；*vt.* 滥用

用 be abused by… 被……滥用

the abuse of… 滥用……

abuse a privilege 滥用特权

abuse one's authority 滥用权力

abuse of power 滥用权力

alcohol abuse that 酗酒，滥用酒精

例 However, many people fear that the good will and generosity are being abused by some governments. 但是很多人担心善意和慷慨的捐助会被有些政府利用。

stand by 坐视不管，袖手旁观

同 look on with folded arms 袖手旁观

sit by 坐视不管，无动于衷

例 Civilised men cannot stand by while other people are struggling in poverty and misery. 当别人在贫困和痛苦中挣扎的时候，文明人是不会袖手旁观的。

restricted [ris'triktid] *adj.* 限制的，限定的，受约束的

拓 restriction *n.* 限制，约束；restrict *vt.* 受限制

用 be restricted to… 局限于……

例 A growing number of environmental problems are no longer restricted to a certain region or country.
越来越多的环境问题已经不再局限于某个国家或地区了。

写作提示

restrict可用于被动语态中。常用于烟草是否被禁止，媒体里的电视网络、游戏是否受限，媒体中犯罪细节是否受限等话题。

be subject to 受支配，从属于；常遭受……

同 be attached to 隶属于，附属于，从属于

例 Private donations, especially large philanthropic donations can be subject to political or economic goals or subject to special interest.
私人的捐助，尤其是大量的慈善捐助，要受政治或经济目的的制约，或是受特殊利益的支配。

materially [mə'tiəriəli] *adv.* 物质上

用 materially and spiritually 物质上和精神上

例 For they can materially shape develop-ment in the poor world, wealthy nations should consist largely of providing resources to and trading opportunities for poor countries.
富国可以从物质上改变穷国的发展，所以他们应该提供大量的资源及贸易机会。

grant [grɑ:nt] *vt.* 授予；承认；允许；*n.* 授予物，拨款

用 assistance on grant terms 援助补助金
basic educational opportunity grant [美]大学生助学金

birth grant 出生许可

例 It aims to reduce poverty by providing interest-free credits and grants for programmes that boost economic growth, reduce inequalities and improve people's living conditions.
它旨在通过零利息和拨款项目来促进经济发展，减少不平等现象及改善人们的生活条件。

disperse [dis'pə:s] *vt.* 使散开，分散，传播；*vi.* 分散

用 disperse assistance 给予援助
disperse the crowd 驱散人群
disperse knowledge 传播知识

例 He urged Congress to give the government greater flexibility in dispersing assistance. 他呼吁议会给予政府在援助别国上更多的灵活性。

burden ['bə:dən] *vt.* 烦扰，使负担；*n.* 重负

用 lighten the burden of... 减轻……的负担
financial burden 经济压力

例 According to the scientific consensus, the climatic change will disproportionately burden developing countries. 气候变化会增加发展中国家的负担，这一点已在科学上达成统一认识。

spur [spə:] *vi.* 给予刺激；*vt.* 激励，鞭策

同 urge *vt.* 推进；stimulate *vt.* 刺激，鼓舞

例 Wealthy countries can spur technological advances that serve the specific interests of developing countries. 富国应该促进科技的发展，为发展中国家的利益服务。

plight [plait] *n.* 困境，境况

同 difficulty *n.* 困难
predicament *n.* 尴尬的处境，困境，窘境

dilemma *n.* 困境，进退两难

用 in the plight 在困境中

例 Developed countries should not abandon the poor to their plight.
发达国家不应该放弃困境中的贫困国家。

yield [ji:ld] *vt.* 出产

例 If aid is increased and delivered more efficiently and trade inequities are addressed, the development will yield rewards. 如果不断增加有效援助，并且解决不平等的贸易问题，那么发展就会开花结果。

open up 打开，开发，开拓

用 open up new market 开拓新市场

例 Other courses of action—such as giving poor nations better economic policy, and more financing new development-friendly technologies, and opening up labor markets—could have more significant benefits. 其他方法，如给穷国更好的经济政策，更多的环保科技支持及开放的劳动力市场，都会带来更多的益处。

direct [dai'rekt] *vt.* 指向，管理；*vi.* 指导，指挥

例 It is time to direct the attention of the world's wealthiest countries to other ways of helping the poorest—ways that have been for too long neglected. 由于富国从其他方面援助贫困国家这一问题被长期忽略，所以现在是时候引导富国了。

intention [in'tenʃən] *n.* 意图，目的，意向

例 The international community must ask itself what really matters for development, so that good intentions can be translated into real benefits for the poorest countries. 国际社会应该明白什么对于发

展是至关重要的，这样才能将对贫困国家的善意转化为穷国的实质利益。

eradicate [i'rædikeit] *vt.* 根除，消灭

拓 eradication *n.* 消灭，根除
eradicative *adj.* 消灭的，根除的

同 exterminate *vt.* 消灭，根除；eliminate *vt.* 消除，排除
get rid of 摆脱，除去

用 eradicate extreme poverty and hunger
消除极度贫穷和饥荒

例 International aid enhances people's living standard and eradicates poverty in the poor countries. 国际援助能够提高贫困国家人们的生活水平，消除贫困。

链接机经关键词

◉ 国际旅游

- 国家之间应增进相互了解(enhance mutual understanding)，促进文化交流 (promote cultural exchange)。
- 对于本国，国际旅游能促进旅游资源的开发(exploit tourist resources)、创造就业机会 (create job opportunities)、促进相关产业发展(promote the relative industries)，具体来说，旅游业的兴起能带动航空业的发展(The surge of the aviation industry prompted by expanding tourism has already brought considerable benefits.)。增加税收 (increase the tax revenue)、提高生活水平 (improve the living standard)、 提升城市在世界的形象和地位(build up the image and status in the world)。
- 对于个人来说，国际旅游能开阔人们的视野

(broaden one's horizons)并丰富人生经验 (enrich one's experience)。

- 有害的一面：对旅游资源的过度开发(over-exploitation of tourist resources)、破坏生态环境(impair the ecological environment)、破坏野生动物的栖息地 (destroy the habitats of the wildlife)、过度消耗自然资源 (over-consume the natural resources)。
- 游客要尽量做到在美好的自然环境和文化环境中，带走的只有照片和记忆(take nothing but pictures and memory)、不要留下涂鸦污染(graffiti pollution)，也不要故意破坏文物(vandalism)，同时要支持当地环保工作(support local environmental and conservation efforts)。
- 文化的融合(cultural assimilation)不代表是一种文化入侵(be regarded as encroachment on the tradition)，而是对文化的丰富(enrichment)。

国际援助

- 出于人道主义(humanitarianism)，援助国(donors/donating countries)对贫困国家(needy countries/poverty-stricken countries/impoverished countries/underdeveloped countries)实施国际援助(international aid/assistance)，例如给予物质援助(beneficence/donation)等，帮助受助国家(recipient countries)摆脱贫困(shake off the poverty)解除困苦(relieve the sufferings)。
- 国际援助的意义

  发扬人道主义精神(humanitarian aid)，帮助贫困国家提高生活水平(living standard)和科技水平(technical level)；缩小贫富差距(bridge the gap of the rich and the poor)，寻求全世界共同发展(seek the common development)。

为受灾的人提供救助(relief)是尊重生命的体现(show respect for life)。有利于促进和平和稳定(peace and security)，促进文化、经济、社会的交流(cultural, economic and social interaction)，促进全球文明的发展(global civilisation)。缓和紧张关系(ease/relieve tension)，让一些国家可以融入全球经济(involvement in the global economy)，促进和平稳定(peace and stability)。

- 国际援助的弊端

被援助国的经济依赖(the poorer countries' economic reliance/dependence)，一些国家会比以往更依靠援助(more dependent on aid than ever)。被援助国的经济依赖会有损其自信(erode self-confidence)、创造力(creativity)和国民的尊严(pride and dignity)。存在滥用援助物资的潜在危险(There exists a potential danger of the abuse of the beneficence by some corrupt governmental officials and in efficient administration.)。

7. 社会与生活题材

考点回顾

A类题目

20130119 照顾孩子是社会最重要的事

20130406 人类进步的领域

20121011 个人快乐与金钱之间的关系

20100220 经济发展与社会价值的丢失

20090611 外地食品与本地食品
G类题目
20130323 现在与过去孩子的健康状况对比
20100605 老年人退休
20100520 成年人的责任
20100410 独立生活

fatherhood ['fɑːðəhud] *n.* 父亲的身份，父权，父性，父道

例 Fatherhood ought to be emphasised as much as motherhood. 父亲应该和母亲同等重要。

maternal instinct 母性本能

例 The sight of the helpless little boy aroused her maternal instinct.
那孤苦无助的小男孩激发了她的母性。

bring up 抚养，养育；培养，教育

同 breed *vt.* 养育；教育； nurture *vt.* 养育
raise *vt.* 养育

用 bring up a new generation 培养一代新人

例 The idea that women are solely responsible for deciding whether or not to have babies leads on to the idea that they are also responsible for bringing the children up.
谈到女性有决定是否要孩子的权利时，就不得不谈到她们也有抚养孩子的义务。

raise [reiz] *vt.* 养育（子女）

例 If parents could raise their children to be considerate of others and to be social, responsible individuals, the whole community would benefit. 如果家长在抚养小孩的过程中让小孩学会尊重他人、成为有责任感的人，那么整个社会都会因此受益。

child-rearing [tʃaild,riəriŋ] *n.* 抚养子女

用 child-rearing pattern 育儿模式

例 I believe that child-rearing should be the responsibility of both parents and that, whilst the roles within that partnership may be different, they are nevertheless equal in importance.

我认为抚养子女是父母共同的职责，虽然父母在与孩子的关系中扮演的角色可能不同，但却是同等重要的。

parenting role 家长的角色

例 Thus, while it is all very well to suggest a greater role for men in raising children, let's not forget that women are generally better suited to the parenting role.

因此，尽管提倡男性在抚育孩子上发挥更大的作用固然不错，但是我们也不要忘记女性总体来说更适合家长的角色。

role-model [rəul'mɔdl] *n.* 榜样，崇拜对象

用 look at sth./sb. as a role-model 把某人/某事当做榜样

例 However, this does not mean that the traditional family, with both parents providing emotional support and role-models for their children, is not the most satisfactory way of bringing up children.

然而，这并不是说父母共同给孩子情感支持、做孩子榜样的传统家庭不是抚养孩子最令人满意的方式。

Electra complex 恋父情结

拓 Oedipus complex 恋母情结

single parent 单身父（或母）亲

用 single parent family 单亲家庭

例 In some places, it has been made easier over the years

for single parents to raise children on their own.
在一些地方，这些年单身父母独自抚养孩子变得简单一些了。

domestic [də'mestik] *adj.* 家庭的

同 household *adj.* 家庭的

用 domestic life 家庭生活
domestic violence 家庭暴力

例 To make the domestic life a happy one both husband and wife must mutually fulfill their duties by each other.
想要家庭生活幸福，夫妻两人必须都要履行对彼此的责任。

financial support 经济支援，财政支援

同 economic support 经济支援

用 provide the financial support 提供经济支援

例 At its simplest, it could mean giving the financial support necessary to provide a home, food and clothes and making sure the child is safe and receives an adequate education.
简单来说就是提供经济支持：养家、买食品和衣服、确保孩子安全并能接受充分的教育。

peer group 同龄人，同辈人

拓 peer pressure 同龄人的压力

例 The peer group has become television-oriented, arid much of the time children spend together is occupied by watching television.
同龄人的聚会都是围着电视转，孩子们在一起的大多数时间都是在看电视。

pass on 传递，传承

同 hand down 传承

用 pass on... to 把……传给（下一代）

例 Parents want to pass on their values to their children. However, things change. The children of today are growing up in a world different from their parents'. 父母期望能将他们的价值观传承下去。然而，事情是变化的，今天的孩子生活在一个与他们父母不同的世界里。

comportment [kəm'pɔːtmənt] *n.* 举止，态度，动作

同 behaviour *n.* 行为，习性；manner *n.* 方式，行为
deportment *n.* 举止

例 To be sure, parents have always been concerned about their children's well-being, independence and comportment.
诚然，家长们总是很关注自己的孩子是否健康快乐、是否独立和行为举止是否得当。

conditioning [kən'diʃəniŋ] *n.* 条件作用

例 Women have proven themselves superior parents as a result of their conditioning, their less aggressive nature and their generally better communication skills.
女性自身的条件，不强势的天性及良好的沟通技巧证明了她们（比男性）更容易做一个好家长。

be preferable to 比……更好

例 Obviously, in raising children, a more patient, gentle manner is preferable to a more aggressive one.
很显然，在抚养孩子方面，有耐心、温和的个性要比强势的个性更好。

resort to 诉诸；依靠；求助于

用 resort to arms 诉诸武力
resort to violence 采用暴力

例 By and large, females are less likely to resort to violence in attempting to solve problems. 总的来说，女性不太可能诉诸暴力来解决问题。

kinship ['kinʃip] *n.* 亲属关系，家属关系；亲密关系

用 kinship family 大家庭

kinship relationship 亲属关系

blood kinship 血缘关系

例 The importance of bonds of kinship is gradually fading from their minds.

亲属关系的重要性在他们的脑海里慢慢淡化了。

nuclear family 核心家庭

例 The children stay in the nuclear family until they grow up and marry.

孩子们在长大结婚之前都会与父母住在一起。

extended family 大家庭（与祖父母、已婚子女等共居的三代或数代同堂的家庭）

例 Many of life problems are beyond the capability of the extended family to resolve.

现在，很多生活问题不是大家庭能解决的了。

背景补充

现代社会的家庭模式主要有以下三种。（1）核心家庭，a nuclear family—two adults and their children, 即由父母亲和他们的孩子构成，这是一些国家流行的家庭模式。（2）大家庭，an extended family, 由祖父母和其他亲戚组成的一个大家族，这种模式在一些发展中国家和农村非常盛行。（3）单亲家庭，a single-parent family，孩子与离异的父亲或者母亲生活的家庭，或者是未婚母亲与子女的家庭。

family ties 家庭关系

拓 feed/raise/support a family 抚养家庭

found/start a family 建立家庭

family property 家产

family financial situation 家境

family tree 家谱

family origin 家庭出身

family responsibilities 家庭责任

family relationship 家庭关系

family education 家庭教育

family structure 家庭结构

family ethics 家庭伦理

同 family bonds 家庭纽带

用 strengthen family ties 加强家庭关系

例 Eastern societies traditionally value educating and family ties, attaching great importance to the upbringing of their young.

东方国家传统上重视教育，同时也有强烈的家庭观念。在这个基础上，抚养子女异常重要。

generation gap 代沟（两代人之间的隔阂）

用 narrow the generation gap 缩小代沟

bridge the generation gap 消弭代沟

例 Mutual understanding is a good way to bridge the generation gap.

相互了解是消弭代沟的好方法。

intergenerational [ˌintə(ː)ˌdʒenəˈreiʃənl] *adj.* 两代间的

例 Intergenerational cold war will be ended one day by tearing down the walls that have been erected between young and old in recent decades. 年轻人和老年人近年来因代沟而引发的冷战终有一天会结束。

pension ['penʃən] *n.* 养老金，退休金，津贴；*vt.* 给予……养老金等

同 stipend *n.* 定期津贴，养老金； allowance *n.* 津贴
subsidy *n.* 津贴，补助金

用 live on pension 靠养老金生活
pension insurance 养老保险

例 He was pensioned by the employer and has departed from the company.
他已拿着公司给他的养老金离开了公司。

reconcile ['rekənsail] *vt.* 调解，调停

同 harmonize *vt.* 使和谐；*vi.* 协调，和谐

用 reconcile with… 与……和解
reconcile (oneself) to
使（自己）甘心于，安于，使能适应

例 The teacher in charge of our class had to reconcile disputes among the students.
我们的班主任必须调解学生间的纠纷。

compromise ['kɔmprəmaiz] *vt.&vi.* 妥协，和解；*n.* 妥协

同 concede *vt.* 退让；*vi.* 让步

用 strike a compromise 达成妥协
compromise with sb. on sth. 在某事上向某人妥协

例 I am prepared to make some concession on minor details, but I can't compromise on fundamentals.
在一些细节上我可以有些让步，但在基本原则上不会妥协。

remove misunderstandings 消除误会

例 To remove misunderstandings, the young should learn as much as possible from the old; similarly, the old should also march forward with the young who have many fresh ideas.

为消除误会，年轻人要尽量多向长辈学习；同样，因为年轻人拥有很多新奇的想法，长辈们也应该和年轻人一同跟上时代的步伐。

friction ['frikʃən] *n.*（因意见分歧、急躁等而产生的）不和，争执，摩擦

同 conflict *n.* 冲突，矛盾

disagreement *n.* 不一致，争论，意见不同

用 generational friction 代际间的摩擦

family friction 家庭中的摩擦

例 They can't know deeply about each other, and then friction is easy to turn up. 他们不能够深入地了解对方，所以很容易出现摩擦。

smooth communication 顺畅的沟通

例 The disagreement and friction often take place between the two generations if they do not have the smooth communication.

如果两代人无法顺畅沟通，他们之间的争端与摩擦就会时有发生。

obedient [ə'biːdjənt] *adj.* 孝顺的，顺从的，服从的

同 submissive *adj.* 顺从的，服从的

compliant *adj.* 顺从的，服从的

用 be obedient to 服从

例 That parents ask their children to be obedient to them is also one of the causes of generation gap between them. 父母要求孩子服从于他们也是导致代沟的原因之一。

alienation [ˌeiliə'neiʃən] *n.*（感情上的）疏远，离间，冷漠

拓 alienate *vt.* 使疏远；alienated *adj.*（被）疏远的

用 create alienation between people

造成人与人之间的疏远

例 Alcoholism often leads to the alienation of family and friends.
酗酒常常导致家庭和朋友间的关系疏远。

become estranged from… 与……疏远

拓 estrangedness *n.* 离间，疏远
estrangement *n.* 疏远

同 become alienated from… 和……疏远

例 Many children have to leave their parents at an early age to study or work elsewhere. As time passes, children become emotionally estranged from their parents.
许多孩子很小就离开父母去外地学习或工作。随着时间推移，他们在感情上与父母疏远。

cultural change 文化变迁

例 Because of more rapid cultural change during the modern era, differences between the two generations increase in comparison to previous times, particularly with respect to such matters as musical tastes, fashion, culture and politics.
由于现代快速的文化变迁，与以往相比，两代人之间在音乐、时尚和文化的品位上以及在政治想法上的分歧越来越多。

social circles 社交圈子

例 Children increasingly rely on personal technological devices like cellphones to create social circles apart from their families, changing the way they communicate with their parents.
孩子们越来越依赖像手机这样的私人电子设备来扩大除了家人之外的社会圈子，这从而也就改变了与父母的沟通方式。

social values 社会价值

例 American adults from young to old disagree increasingly today on social values ranging from religion to interpersonal relationships.
美国的年轻人和老年人在社会价值上（从宗教到人际关系）存在的分歧日益增多。

privy ['privi] *adj.* 私人的，不公开的

同 private *adj.* 私人的

用 privy to 参与，知情

例 Cellphones give teens more of a private life. Their parents are not privy to all of their conversations.
手机让青少年有了更多的隐私，家长们没有权利知道孩子所有的谈话内容。

be likely to do 倾向于做，很有可能做

同 tend to do 往往，倾向于

例 Younger people are more likely to embrace technology.
年轻人更容易接受新科技。

egoistic [ˌiːgəu'istik] *adj.* 自私自利的，以自我为中心的

拓 egoistically *adv.* 任性地，自私地
egoistical *adj.* 自私自利的
egoism *n.* 利己主义
ego defense 自我防卫
ego expansion 自我扩张
ego instinct 自我本能
egocentric *adj.* 以自我为中心的
egocentricity *n.* 自我中心
egocentrism *n.* 唯我主义

同 self-centred *adj.* 以自我为中心的
selfish *adj.* 自私的

例 An egoistic person can not love.
一个以自我为中心的人不能爱。

misconduct [ˌmisˈkɔndʌkt] *n.* 不端行为，处理不当；*vt.* 处理不当，行为不检

同 misbehaviour *n.* 品行不端，不礼貌
wrongdoing *n.* 坏事，不道德的行为

用 misconduct oneself 行为不端

例 These men misconducted themselves in the hall with loud talk. 这些人在大厅里大声说话，表现恶劣。

rebellious [riˈbeliəs] *adj.* 反抗的，造反的，不服管教的

拓 rebel *vi.* 反叛；*n.* 反叛者
rebelliously *adv.* 难以控制地，造反地
rebelliousness *n.* 造反，叛逆性

同 defiant *adj.* 挑衅的，蔑视的，挑战的
resistant *adj.* 抵抗的，反抗的

例 Keep your mind calm and serene; your own real enemy is your own rebellious mind. 心灵要保持和平清净；你真正的敌人是你浮躁的心。

behaviour [biˈheivjə] *n.* 行为，举止，态度

拓 misbehaviour *n.* 品行不端，不礼貌
well-behaved *adj.* 行为端正的

同 manner *n.* 方式，行为

例 Poor student behaviour seems to be an increasingly widespread problem and I think that modern lifestyles are probably responsible for this.
学生行为不端的现象日益严重，我认为原因在于现代的生活方式。

spoil [spɔil] *vt.* 溺爱

拓 spoilt *adj.* 宠坏的

同 dote *vt.&vi.* 溺爱

用 be badly spoilt 被惯坏

例 These children are often spoilt, not in terms of love and attention because working parents do not have the time for this, but in more material ways.
孩子经常被大人溺爱，这并不意味着他们得到了充分的关爱和关怀，而是父母因为外出工作没有那么多的时间陪伴他们的孩子，所以只能在物质方面给予他们充分的满足。

consideration [kənˌsidəˈreiʃən] *n.* 考虑

拓 considerate *adj.* 体谅的，考虑周到的
considerable *adj.* 重要的，值得考虑的；相当大的

用 take into consideration 考虑
under consideration 在考虑中

例 This means that the children grow up without consideration for others and without any understanding of where their standard of living comes from. 这意味着这些孩子在成长的过程中，没有学会为他人考虑，也不知道自己所享受的生活是谁创造的。

respect [risˈpekt] *vt.&n.* 尊敬，敬重

拓 respectful *adj.* 恭敬的，有礼貌的
respectfully *adv.* 尊敬地
self- respect *n.* 自重

用 show respect for 对……表示尊敬
with respect 怀有敬意

例 They have less respect for their teachers and refuse to obey school rules.
他们不那么尊敬老师，也不愿意遵守学校的规章制度。

lie with 取决于，在于

同 depend upon (on) 信赖，依靠；rely on 信赖，依靠

用 the solution lies with… 解决方法在于……

例 But I think the solution lies with the families, who need to be more aware of the future consequences of spoiling their children.

但我认为虽然问题发生在学校，但解决方法却在家庭，因为家庭需要更加明白溺爱儿童会造成的后果。

genetic [dʒi'netik] *adj.* 遗传的，基因的；起源的

用 genetic factor 遗传因素

例 Today the way we consider human psychology and mental development is heavily influenced by the genetic sciences.

现在我们认为人类心理和心智发育受基因学的影响很大。

inherit [in'herit] *vt.* 继承，遗传而得；*vi.* 成为继承人

拓 inheritable *adj.* 会遗传的，可继承的

inheritance *n.* 遗产，继承

inheritor *n.* 继承人，后继者

用 inherit from… 从……继承

例 Children should be educated to inherit the glorious revolutionary tradition.

我们应该教育孩子继承光荣的革命传统。

trait [treit] *n.* 特性，特征；性格，品质

同 quality *n.* 质量，品质，特性

用 traits of character 性格特征

personality trait 个性品质

例 Instead, the traits we inherited from our parents and experiences that we encounter in life are constantly interacting. 相反，我们从父母那里继承的特质与我们在生活中的经历相互影响。

birth rate 出生率

用 restrict the birth rate 限制出生率

例 In many countries, the birth rate is decreasing so that families are smaller with fewer children.
在许多国家，由于出生率的下降，家庭规模越来越小。

please [pli:z] *vt.* 使高兴，使满意，使喜欢；
vi. 令人高兴，讨人喜欢

用 please every customer 热心地对待每一位顾客

例 They are allowed to have whatever they want, regardless of price, and to behave as they please.
不管价格高低，孩子想要什么就能得到什么，而且做事情随心所欲。

self-control [ˌselfkən'trəul] *n.* 克己，自我控制

例 When they get to school age, these children have not learnt any self-control or discipline.
这些孩子在上学之前没有任何自制力，也没有纪律观念。

retirement [ri'taiəmənt] *n.* 退休

拓 retire *vi.&vt.* 退休； retired *adj.* 退休的

用 go into retirement 退休
live in retirement 过退休的生活
retirement age 退休年龄
retirement allowance 退休金
retirement pension 退休金
retirement home 养老院
retirement pensioner 靠退休金生活的人
mandatory retirement 强制退休

例 Our elder population was encouraged by media to view the retirement years as a time for self-indulgence and total relaxation. 媒体上一直提倡老年人应享受完全放松的退休生活。

demographic [deməˈgræfik] *adj.* 人口统计学的，人口学的

用 demographic structure 人口结构

demographic census 人口普查

例 A massive demographic shift in China is under way. 中国正在经历一场巨大的人口结构变革。

graying population 人口老龄化

例 If European nations want to preserve their generous social security system in an age of graying population, it can only be done by economic growth.

在人口老龄化的时代，如果欧洲国家要继续维持慷慨大方的社会福利体系，那么它们只能靠经济增长来实现。

写作提示

常考话题：(1) 人口老龄化对社会的利弊影响；(2) 人们不尊重老人的原因以及影响；(3)老人的传统观念对于年轻人是否还有指导意义。

解决措施：要发挥政府的保障和引导作用(take proper support and guidance)；建立社会保障体系并完善医疗系统(establish social security system and perfect medical system)；修建娱乐与健身设施(build entertainment and fitness facilities)；调动家庭和社会力量的积极性(bring one's initiative into full play)；建立社区诊所(make community clinics available)；引导老年人适当就业(provide them with employment opportunities)；建立灵活的退休制度(flexible retirement policies)；老年人角色的新定位(defining new roles for older adults and civic engagement)；投资于终生学习(invest in life long learning)。

senior ['siːniə] *adj.* 年老的，年长的，资格较老的，资历较深的

例 Despite the advantages of early retirement, I strongly believe that it is better for senior workers to continue working as long as they are physically and mentally capable. 尽管提前退休有诸多好处，但我还是坚持认为只要老年人身心健康，继续工作对他们来说是最好的选择。

senior citizens 年长公民，老年公民，老年人（尤指65岁以上者或已退休者）

同 the elderly 老年人； the aged 老年人

例 Communities will play an important role in senior citizens' care, tending their physical, psychological and medical needs.
社区应通过多种方式为老年人提供生活照料、精神慰藉和卫生服务。

seasoned citizen 经验丰富的公民；老年人

例 Seasoned citizens Days at Sandy Cove include inspiring Christian music and a message, with a delicious luncheon for senior adults ages 55 and over.
在桑地海湾举行的老人节上将会有鼓舞人心的基督教音乐和按摩，并为55岁以上的老年人提供美味的午餐。

背景补充

seasoned citizen本义是“经验丰富的公民，饱经风霜的公民”，其委婉义是“老年人”，一般指55岁以上的老人，seasoned citizen也可以说seasoned man或seasoned people，其中，seasoned表示“久经历练的、饱经风霜的”，因此，带有褒奖之意。

burnt-out ['bə:ntaut] *adj.* 疲倦不堪的

同 exhausted *adj.* 耗尽的，疲惫的

weary *adj.* 疲倦的，厌烦的

fatigued *adj.* 疲乏的

worn out 疲惫不堪的

例 The project went on for over two years and by the end of it I was just burnt-out.

工程足足进行了两年多，到最后我精疲力竭。

maintain [mein'tein] *vt.* 维持，维修

同 keep *vt.&vi.* 保持

例 A close family relationship can surely be maintained as long as we realise the significant role it plays in our lives and attach importance to it.

只要我们意识到并重视良好家庭关系的重要性，那么肯定就能维持融洽的家庭关系。

reach a certain age 达到一定的年龄

例 Thus, workers who can still demonstrate their capacity to carry out their work should not be asked to retire simply because they have reached a certain age.

因此，对于在工作中仍能发挥才能的人，不要仅仅因为他们到了一定年龄就要求他们退休。

in the name of 以……名义

用 in the name of love 以爱的名义

例 Parents may be too close to their children emotionally. For example, they may limit a child's freedom in the name of safety. 家长有时对孩子看得太紧，可能以安全的名义限制孩子的自由。

breadwinner ['bred,winə] *n.*养家糊口的人

例 However, even though we mentioned the fact that

growing numbers of women are working outside the home, the father is still thought by many people as the breadwinner in the household.

然而，即使现在越来越多的女性在外工作，很多人仍然认为父亲是家庭中养家糊口的人。

背景补充

bread就是面包，面包是美国人和欧洲人的基本食品，就像亚洲国家许多人每天吃米饭一样。面包对西方人来说是非常重要的。在有些俗语或谚语当中，bread这个字被用来代表钱(money)。这就可以说明bread的重要性了。breadwinner实际上是由两个词合起来的，bread和winner，breadwinner从字面上来理解，它的意思就是：赢得面包的人，解释为：家里主要挣钱的人，也就是养家糊口的人。以往，breadwinner一般都是家庭里面的男人来承担，但是，现在情况已经有了变化，越来越多的妇女加入了劳动大军。

shuttle [ˈʃʌtl] *vt.&vi.* 穿梭，往返

用 shuttle back and forth between work and family

往返于工作和家庭之间

例 Some working ladies have to shuttle back and forth between work and family, which is not easy to strike a balance between them.

职业女性每天往返于工作和家庭之间，想在这两者之间达到平衡是很难的。

gender discrimination 性别歧视

例 Gender discrimination is one of the most traditional, widespread, and serious types of employment discrimination in the labour market.

性别歧视是劳动力市场最传统、最普遍、最严重的就业歧视之一。

tempo ['tempəu] *n.* 速度；拍子

用 quick tempo 快速；slow tempo 慢速

例 The tempo of life has accelerated.
生活节奏日益加快。

telecommute [ˌtelikə'mju:t] *vi.* （利用电脑终端机）远距离工作

拓 telecommuter *n.* 远程工作者

例 Many people want to telecommute, for it saves the time and cost of travelling to and from work.
但是许多人希望远程办公，因为这样节省路上的时间和坐车的费用。

lack of 没有，缺乏，不足

用 lack of communication 缺乏沟通

例 Lack of relax may partly contribute to their sub-health, like the tooth decay, strains and aches and others too numerous to list.
休息不足可能导致亚健康，例如龋齿、精神紧张、疼痛等等。

链接机经关键词

⊙ 社会老龄化(aging society)

世界步入老龄化(the world is aging)，老年人(the elderly/senior citizen/the aged/the old)的比例增大。

由于医疗条件的改善和生活水平的提高(social security and medical treatment)，人们寿命增长(Life span is longer than before.)。

社会老龄化带来的问题：

由于老年人劳动能力下降(decrease in effective

working force)，很多老年人依赖养老金生活(live on pension)，增加了政府的负担(take up the duty of caring for the aged members)。

老龄化社会解决之道：

加强家庭联系(consolidate the family ties)，给老人精神安慰(spiritual comfort)；

社区应多为老年人服务(encourage the community service for the aged)。

退休(retirement)

正面影响：能够使老年人放松(relax in retirement)，为年轻人提供就业机会(open up opportunities for younger people to get into the workforce)。

负面影响：老年人退休会导致他们觉得自己没用(useless)，被社会淘汰(mean to be sifted out)，这在很多情况下会导致心理问题(suffer from certain mental problems)；老年人在某一领域往往是专业人士(specialist)，退休意味着资源的流失(loss of the labour resources)；增加了社会福利成本(social welfare cost)。

代沟(generation gap)

代沟是不同年龄段人之间的差异(Generation gap means the "distinction" between the old and the young.)。代沟源于缺乏理解和沟通(derive from a lack of understanding and communication)。成年人和年轻人之间的代沟很难缓解(Generation gap between the grown-ups and the young remains unbridged.)。缩小代沟(narrow the gap/bridge the gap)就要消除误解(remove the misunderstanding)，互相包容(tolerance)。

8. 政府政策题材

考点回顾

20100417 政府倡导健康的生活方式
20091031 与政府相关的环境话题
20090704 科研投资

general public 公众

用 raise the general public's awareness of…
提升公众……的意识

例 I think, therefore, that governments need to raise this awareness in the general public. 因此我认为政府应该提高公众的意识。

写作提示

作文中的人称主语可选择像individual, people, human race, humanity, man, humankind, the public, 主要是为了达到客观性的描述，尽量减少主观色彩。

fund [fʌnd] *n.* 资金，基金，存款；*vt.* 投资；资助

用 publicly-funded health care 公共医疗
a state-funded program 政府提供资金的项目

例 The government should fund this kind of parental support, because this is no longer a problem for individual families, but for the society as a whole.
政府应该资助家庭教育，因为这不再是每个家庭自己的问题，也是全社会的问题。

public purse 国库，公共资金

同 national treasury 国库

例 The children should be entitled to receive financial aid from public purse. 孩子有权利享受国家经济援助。

in dispute 在争论中，处于争议中

同 at/in issue 处于争议中

例 The problem that who is responsible for paying university tuition fees has been in dispute for many years. 关于谁来承担大学学费的问题，多年来一直备受争议。

in the interest of 符合……的利益

用 be in the interest of whole society
符合全社会的利益

例 A long term relationship between the US and China based on mutual trust, respect and benefit is undoubtedly in the interest of China, the US and indeed the world. 中美的长远关系建于互相信任、互相尊重和互惠互利的基础上，绝对符合中国、美国和全世界的利益。

be sponsored by 由……发起；由……赞助

同 be supported by 由……支持

例 Education and medical service are supposed to be sponsored by both government and public funds. 教育和公共医疗应该由政府基金和公共基金共同承担。

understandable [ˌʌndəˈstændəbl] *adj.* 可以理解的

拓 understanding *n.* 理解
misunderstanding *n.* 误解，误会

例 It is certainly very understandable that some governments should start looking at ways of limiting their populations to a sustainable figure.

非常可以理解的是政府应该考虑一下将人口控制在合理范围内的方法。

regulate ['regjuleit] *vt.* 调节；规定；管理，控制

拓 regulation *n.* 规则，管理

用 regulate the expenditure 控制开支

regulate daily life 使日常生活规律化

sth. is regulated by... 某事物由……调控

例 In the past, populations were regulated by frequent war and widespread disease, but in recent years the effects of those factors have been diminished.

过去，频繁的战争和疾病的传播能控制住人口的数量，近些年来这些方面的因素减少了。

feed extra mouth 养活额外的人口

例 Countries can be faced with a population that is growing much faster than the nation's food resources or employment opportunities and whose members can be condemned to poverty by the need to feed extra mouths. 国家可能会面临食物和就业机会无法满足人口迅猛增长的局面，人们可能就会因为这些额外的人口而陷入贫困。

identify [ai'dentifai] *vt.* 把……看作一致；辨认，识别

用 identify...with... 使等同于

identify...as... 认为……是……

例 They identify population control as a measure to raise living standards.

他们认为控制人口是提高生活水平的一项措施。

compulsion [kəm'pʌlʃən] *n.* 强迫，强制，强制力

拓 compulsive *adj.* 强制的，强迫的

compulsively *adv.* 强制地，强迫地

用 under (upon, on) compulsion 被迫地

do sth. by persuasion rather than compulsion
通过劝导而非强制来做某事

例 For that reason, it would seem that the best approach would be to work by persuasion rather than compulsion.
出于这个原因，最好的解决途径应该是劝导，而非强制。

写作提示

雅思写作常用到do sth. by persuasion rather than compulsion的句型，既提出建议，又有折中的意味，如家庭话题中父母教育孩子的话题，应该以劝导和教育为主，而不能体罚孩子(corporal punishment或者physical punishment)；如新任教师和医生是否应该到落后地区工作：Some people think new teachers and doctors should work in rural areas for a few years, but others think everyone should be free to choose the place in which they work. 可以提出类似的解决方案：The best solution is not to order, but to encourage or persuade. 这样的思路使文章既能达到一种客观平衡，又符合事实，所以记住persuasion rather than compulsion这个实用的短语吧！

preferred [priˈfəːd] *adj.* 首选的，优先的

拓 prefer *vt.* 宁愿；*vi.* 愿意；preferable *adj.* 更好的

用 preferred customers 有优先权的顾客

例 This is the preferred way. 这是首选的方法。

tax incentive 税收鼓励

拓 tax revenue 税收；tax exemption 免税

例 Of course, if this does not succeed within a reasonable time scale, it may be necessary to consider other measures, such as tax incentives or child-benefit payments for small families only. 当然如果在一定时期内该方法不奏效，就要考虑只针对于小家庭的措施，像税收鼓励或孩子补贴之类。

midway ['mid'wei] *n.* 中途，折中办法

例 These are midways between persuasion and compulsion. 这些是在劝导和强制之间的折中办法。

写作提示

雅思作文的结构大致可分为“一边倒式作文”和“折中式作文”，参看考官的范文，我们会发现大多数都是“平衡式写法”，即折中观点较多。那么折中写法的词汇都有哪些？

(1) moderately *adv.* 适当地，适度地，中庸地
in moderation 适度地

(2) relative *adj.* 相对的；relatively *adv.* 相对地

(3) to a large extent 在很大程度上
雅思的题干中经常出现to what extent do you agree or disagree? 即：你在多大程度上同意或者不同意？

(4) to some extent, to some degree 都是表示“从一定程度上说”
句式：To some degree, lack of … contributes to…
在一定程度上，……的缺乏导致了……

(5) partly *adv.* 部分地，在一定程度上

preventive [pri'ventiv] *adj.* 预防的，防止的

同 prevention *n.* 预防

用 preventive action 预防措施
preventive maintenance 预防性维修
preventive measure 防护措施，预防措施

例 That is why, in recent years, there has been a growing body of opinion in favour of putting more resources into health education and preventive measures. 这也就是为什么近些年来有越来越多的人支持将更多的资源投入到健康教育的普及和预防的措施中来。

hygiene ['haidʒi:n] *n.* 卫生学，卫生，保健法

用 hygiene education 卫生教育；保健教育

hygiene of environment 环境卫生

personal hygiene 个人卫生

domestic hygiene 家庭卫生

hygiene regulations 卫生守则

hygiene instruction 卫生教育工作

例 People should wash regularly to ensure personal hygiene. 人们经常洗澡以保证个人卫生。

cost-effectiveness 成本高效益，花费的有效性

例 Statistics demonstrate the cost-effectiveness of treating a condition in the early stages, rather than delaying until more expensive and prolonged treatment is necessary.
有数据表明早期的治疗会提高效益，而如果拖延病情，就需要更昂贵、更长时间的治疗。

budget ['bʌdʒit] *n.* 预算

用 on a budget 避免不必要的开支，节省开支

例 So far so good, but the difficulties start when we try to define what the proportion of the budget should be diverted from treatment.
到目前还好，但是当我们试图确定有多少预算要从医疗上转走时，问题就来了。

health education campaigns 健康教育宣传

例 How do we accurately measure which health education campaigns are effective in both medical and financial terms?
就医疗和经济而言，我们怎么来准确衡量健康教育宣传是否有效呢?

call for 要求，提倡

用 call for time and patience 需要时间和耐心

…is called for, so that… 要号召……，以便……

例 A very rigorous process of evaluation is called for, so that we can make informed decisions.
要提倡严格的评估程序以便我们做出正确的决定。

illiterate [i'litərit] *adj.* 目不识丁的，文盲的；*n.* 文盲，无知

拓 illiteracy *n.* 文盲，无知

同 uneducated *adj.* 未受教育的
ignorant *adj.* 无知的，愚昧的
unlearned *adj.* 无学问的，未受教育的

反 literate *adj.* 受过教育的

用 illiterate population 未受教育的人口

例 When a considerable percentage are illiterate, the whole machinery of government has to take account of the fact. 如果有很多人都是文盲，整个政府机构应该重视这个事实。

have access to 使用；接近；可以利用

例 Governments should make sure that all their citizens have access to a good standard of free education at primary and secondary level. 政府应该确保所有人都能接受小学及中学的免费教育。

available [ə'veiləbl] *adj.* 可利用的，可达到的

例 Therefore, primary and secondary education should be freely available for all if possible but that further education should not necessarily be wholly free.
因此，如果可能的话，小学教育和中学教育应该全部免费，但是高等教育没有必要全免。

betterment ['betəmənt] *n.* 提高，改善，改进

例 The betterment of the medical service is in the interest of the general public.
医疗服务的改善符合大众的利益。

compulsory education 义务教育

例 At present, the most important measure is to carry out compulsory education. 在现阶段，最重要的措施是全面贯彻实施义务教育。

levy ['levi] *vt.&vi.* 征税

用 levy income taxes 征收收入所得税

例 The government levies taxes on real estate and personal property. 政府征收不动产和动产税。

health care services 保健服务

例 Assuring access to safe water and primary health care services are crucial.
确保清洁的饮水和基本医疗服务是很关键的。

provision [prə'viʒən] *n.* 供应，提供；*vt.* 为……提供所需物品（尤指食物）

用 make ample provision for 充裕的供养
make provision against 防备，预防
make provision for
为……采取措施，为……做好准备
run out of provisions 粮食缺乏
short of provisions 粮食缺乏

例 The government is responsible for the provision of education for all the children.
政府有责任让儿童接受教育。

expenditure [iks'penditʃə] *n.* 支出，花费

同 spending *n.* 开销，花费； expense *n.* 开支，消费

用 expenditure for social security 社会保障支出
expenditure pattern 消费模式
expenditure tax 消费支出税

例 One traditional way to do this is to increase government expenditures, probably in public infrastructure projects. 一种传统做法是增加政府支出，这些支出可能是用在公共基础设施项目方面。

shoulder ['ʃəuldə] *vt.* 肩负，承担

同 assume *vt.* 承担； undertake *vt.* 承担，保证

用 shoulder the responsibility/duty 承担责任

例 There has long been a heated discussion about whether the government should shoulder the responsibilities for its people's basic expenses such as health care and education.
政府是否应该为人民承担像医疗与教育方面的费用，很长时间以来一直是人们激烈讨论的话题。

welfare ['welfεə] *n.* 幸福；福利；康乐

用 on welfare 接受救济的，接受生活照顾的
welfare facilities 福利设施
welfare fund 福利基金
welfare system 福利体系
social welfare 社会福利

例 Most of the families in this neighbourhood are on welfare.
这一带的大多数家庭都接受政府的福利救济。

spur [spəː] *vt.* 激励，鞭策

用 spur interest in... 激发在……的兴趣

例 Building theatres and stadiums, which spurs interest in the arts and sports respectively, would be practically identical to spend money on medical care and education.
修建剧院和体育场会激发人们对艺术和运动的兴趣，实际上就相当于在医疗和教育上的投资。

social security 社会保险，社会保障

例 A sound fund management system of social security

for aged is an important part of the social security system, essential assurance of achieving social stability and economic development.
健全的老年社会保障资金管理体制是社会保障体系的重要组成部分，是实现社会稳定和经济发展的必要保证。

medical care 医疗护理

例 The children can get better medical care and education is no longer limited to a small number of people exclusively. 孩子们可以得到更好的医疗保护，并且教育已不再为少数人所专有了。

health insurance 医疗保险

例 This is due to skyrocketing medical cost and the high cost of health insurance. 这是由猛涨的医疗费用和花费很高的医疗保险造成的。

public health 公共卫生

同 public hygiene 公共卫生

例 In fact, smoking bringing damages to the environment and public health is also an undeniable problem.
事实上，吸烟对环境和人体健康的破坏也是一个不可争辩的问题。

public interest 公共利益

例 Personal interest is not always compatible with public interest. 个人利益和公共利益不总是一致的。

administrative [əd'ministrətiv] *adj.* 管理的，行政的

拓 administrate *vt.* 管理，经营
administration *n.* 管理，行政

用 administrative authority 行政当局
administrative management 行政管理

administrative measure 行政措施，行政手段
administrative organization 行政机构，管理机构
administrative penalty 行政处罚
administrative regulation 行政法规
administrative staff 管理人员，行政人员

例 We need to come up with new administrative and legislative measures to restrict new car growth.
我们需要与管理部门和立法机关共同出台新的措施来限制新车增长。

serve the people 为人民服务

例 We must serve the people heart and soul.
我们必须全心全意地为人民服务。

publicity campaigns 宣传运动

用 environmental publicity campaigns 环保宣传运动
anti-drugs publicity campaigns 禁毒宣传运动
conduct publicity campaigns 进行宣传

例 The argument is that ignorance of, for example, basic hygiene or the dangers of an unhealthy diet or lifestyle needs to be combatted by special nationwide publicity campaigns, as well as longer-term health education.
有人认为如果对基础卫生和不健康饮食或生活方式带来的危害一无所知的话，就需要通过全国性的宣传活动以及长期的健康教育来解决了。

链接机经关键词

- 政府职能

政府要全心全意地为人民服务(serve the people heart and soul)，因为人们要交税(tax payment)，政府

应该对纳税人(taxpayers)的公共利益负责(it is the responsibility of the government to be concerned about the public interest)，政府职能体现在以下几方面。

（1）投资艺术领域，可以丰富生活(add spice to people's life)，激发创造性和灵感(stimulate one's creativity and inspiration)；从文化角度来说(in terms of cultural exchange)，增加了向国内外展示文化精粹的平台(a platform to showcase the essence of the civilisation to home and abroad)，同时也是文化交流和传承的平台(pass on the cultural heritage to the next generation)。

（2）提供医疗和社会保障(social security and medical treatment)，健康教育活动(health education health education campaigns—basic hygiene)，享受卫生医疗是人们的一项基本权利(People have a basic right to health-care.)，国家有责任确保从公共预算中提供足够的卫生保健资金(an obligation for the state to ensure adequate health-care resources)。大力发展公共医疗(publicly-funded health care)，有助于疾病预防和基础医疗服务的改善(increased emphasis on preventative and primary health care)。

（3）国家进行义务教育(compulsory educa-tion)可以减轻支付学费的负担(ease the burden of tuition fees)，同时提高文化普及率(raise literacy rate)，但要意识到完全由政府给教育和医疗买单会给政府，尤其是不发达国家带来沉重的负担(might impose much pressure upon a nation economically if governments bear expenses for the higher learning or medical treatment for all the people)。一个合理的解决方法就是由政府基金和公共基金以及家庭共同承担(be sponsored by both government, public funds and family)。

9. 犯罪题材

考点回顾

20100805	青少年犯罪
20100130	分析反社会行为的原因
20090917	将犯罪分子关进监狱还是进行社区服务
20090613	持续犯罪的原因
20080816	是否限制媒体上的犯罪细节

commit crimes 犯罪

拓 crime prevention 预防犯罪；petty crime 轻微犯罪
crack down crime 打击犯罪

例 The research suggests that the majority of criminals who were sent to prison would continue to commit crimes when set free. 研究表明，关进监狱的大部分犯罪分子被释放后还会继续犯罪。

criminal ['kriminəl] *n.* 罪犯；*adj.* 刑事的，犯罪的，罪恶的

用 criminal minds 犯罪心理
criminal motivation 犯罪动机
criminal record 犯罪记录

例 Habitual criminals threaten the public security to a large degree. 惯犯对公共安全有很大的威胁。

crime details 犯罪细节

例 There are now detailed reports about crimes on TV and newspapers. Some people say that crime details should be restricted in the media.

现在电视、报纸会有犯罪细节的报道，有些人认为媒体应该限制这些细节的报道。

juvenile delinquency 青少年犯罪

同 youth crime 青少年犯罪

用 prevention of juvenile delinquency
预防青少年违法犯罪

例 Many of the problems young people now experience, such as juvenile delinquency, arise from the fact that many married women now work and are not at home to care for their children.
现在年轻人面临像青少年犯罪等问题，这是缘于许多已婚女性走进职场，无法在家照看孩子。

crime rate 犯罪率

例 The best way to decrease the crime rate is to extend the period of sentence for criminals.
降低犯罪率最好的方法就是延长罪犯的刑期。

crime-ridden [ˌkraimridən] *adj.* 犯罪猖獗的，充满犯罪行为的

同 full of crimes充满犯罪行为的

例 It is unfriendly, crime-ridden and filled with alcoholics and people who dump trash everywhere.
这是个很不好的地方，犯罪猖獗，酗酒成风，垃圾到处都是。

offender [əˈfendə] *n.* 罪犯；冒犯者；违法者

同 violator *n.* 违背者，违反者； law-breaker *n.* 违法者

用 juvenile offender 青少年罪犯

例 The compassionate judge gave the young offender a light sentence.
慈悲的法官从轻判处了那个年轻罪犯。

violator ['vaiəleitə] *n.* 违背者；违反者；妨碍者

同 law-breaker *n.* 违法者；offender *n.* 罪犯，违法者

例 If the violator causes any property losses or any other damages, the violator shall bear civil liabilities.
造成财产损失或者其他损害的人，应依法承担民事责任。

law-breaker [lɔː'breikə] *n.* 违法者，犯法的人

拓 lawbreaking *adj.* 违反法律的；*n.* 违反法律

同 violator *n.* 违背者，违反者
offender *n.* 罪犯，违法者

例 Some people think law-breakers should be sent to prisons while others claim they should be made to work in communities.
有些人认为违法者应该关进监狱，而另一些人认为他们应该进入社区为人民服务。

infraction [in'frækʃən] *n.* 破坏，违反，违背

同 delinquency *n.* 行为不良，违法犯罪
offense *n.* 犯罪，过错

用 infraction of law 违法
infraction of regulations 违反规则

例 Juveniles, like adults, can be charged with a felony, a misdemeanor, or an infraction.
青少年和成年人一样，可被指控为重罪、行为不端或违法。

truant ['truːənt] *n.* 旷课者；懒惰的人；*vi.* 逃学，偷懒

用 play truant 逃学

例 Children who perform poorly at school are also more likely to truant, which is also linked to offending.
在学校成绩差的孩子们更加容易逃学，这也有可能导致犯罪。

worthlessness ['wə:θlisnis] *n.* 无价值

拓 worth *adj.* 值得……的；有……价值的

worthless *adj.* 无价值的

worthy *adj.* 值得的，有价值的

例 The inability to complete assignments and getting bad grades may create self-esteem problems, feelings of alienation or worthlessness.

不按时完成作业、学习成绩不好就会导致自尊心问题，产生被疏离感或觉得自己毫无价值。

anti-social personality 反社会人格

例 In all abnormal personalities, crimes caused by anti-social personality are the most. 在所有的不正常人格中，反社会人格引起的违法犯罪行为最多。

root cause 根本原因

同 primary cause 主要原因

用 touch the root cause 触及根本原因

potential cause and root cause 潜在原因和根本原因

例 The root causes of crime are many and diverse. Any hope of addressing those causes successfully requires multi-faceted strategies, which can be implemented by neighborhoods, communities and various levels of government. 犯罪的根本原因有很多，要想成功解决问题就要采取多种策略，这需要社区及各级政府的共同努力。

direct cause 直接原因

例 It is certainly true that the position of women in society has undergone a dramatic change in the past twenty years but I do not feel that this is a direct cause of the indisputable increase in juvenile-related problems during this period. 过去二十年间，女性

的地位确实是发生了很大的变化，但是我不认为它是这期间导致与青少年相关问题的原因。

be vulnerable to 易受……的攻击，易受……的侵害

例 Most parents worry that their children are vulnerable to the harmful impact in society. 家长担心的是孩子容易受社会上不良因素的影响。

propensity [prə'pensiti] *n.* 倾向；习性；癖好，偏爱

用 propensity to consume 消费倾向
propensity to invest 投资倾向
have a propensity for sth. 有做某事的倾向

例 These juvenile offenders are in need of treatment because they have a negative disposition and high propensity to continue committing crime. 这些少年犯需要救治，因为他们性情消极，有极大可能继续犯罪。

deviant ['di:viənt] *adj.* 不正常的，离经叛道的；
n. 不正常者，偏常者

同 divergent *adj.* 相异的，分歧的
aberrant *adj.* 脱离常轨的

用 deviant behaviour 异常行为，越轨行为

例 Once labelled as deviant, a young person may accept that role, and be more likely to associate with others who have been similarly labelled. 一旦年轻人被贴上行为异常的标签，他就会接受这个定位，也就更容易和那些志趣相似的人混在一起。

problematic [ˌprɔblə'mætik] *adj.* 成问题的，有疑问的

用 problematic behaviour 有问题的行为
problematic issues 棘手的问题

例 Failure to develop communication skills may lead to more problematic behaviours, such as truancy, running away from home, or more serious acts, such as vandalism, petty theft or violence. 没能掌握良好

的沟通技巧会导致很多不良行为，如逃学、离家出走，或是更严重的行为，如故意破坏他人财产、偷窃或暴力行为。

penalty ['penəlti] *n.* 罚款，处罚

同 punishment *n.* 惩罚； retribution *n.* 报应，惩罚

用 impose heavy penalty on 严惩

pay the penalty 遭受惩罚

the extreme penalty 死刑，极刑

under(on) penalty of 受……的处罚

例 He will receive the penalty for his own behaviour. 他将因自己的所作所为而受到惩罚。

punitive ['pju:nitiv] *adj.* 处罚的，惩罚的

用 punitive measure 惩罚措施

punitive sanction 惩罚性制裁

例 Precise details of how to enforce these punitive measures are still being worked out. 实施这些惩罚措施的具体细节还在进一步讨论之中。

release [ri'li:s] *vt.* 释放，解放；*n.* 释放

同 set free 释放

用 be released from the prison 从狱中被释放

release one's frustrations 发泄不满情绪

release the news 发布新闻

on release（电影）在公映，发行

例 He was released from prison after serving a sentence of five years. 他在服刑五年后从狱中被释放出来。

embark on 开始（工作），着手，从事

用 embark on the criminal road 走上犯罪道路

embark on sth. 开始着手做某事

例 Many young people are misled by the misbehaviour in society and embark on the criminal road.

很多年轻人因为社会上的不良影响而误入歧途，进而走上犯罪的道路。

public safety 公共安全

同 public security 公共安全

例 More and more cameras are being installed, but is public safety really improving?

监视器越装越多，但治安真的有改善吗？

public order 公共秩序，社会治安

同 social order 社会秩序

例 Juvenile delinquency has become a serious social problem to endanger the public order.

少年犯罪已经成为危害社会治安的一个严重的社会问题。

crack down 采取严厉措施，制裁

用 crack down youth crime 降低青年犯罪

crack down on/upon 对……采取严厉措施；制裁

crack down on counterfeit goods 打假

例 The police decided to crack down on drug addicts.

警察决定对吸毒的人采取严厉措施。

uncontrolled [ˌʌnkənˈtrəuld] *adj.* 不受控制的

同 out of control 失去控制

用 go uncontrolled 不加以控制

例 In sum, detailed crime coverage in the media undermines our lives in several ways. I am convinced if such reports continue to go uncontrolled, it will exert even more baneful influence on individuals and societies.

总之，媒体里对于犯罪细节的报道会从几个方面对我们的生活产生负面影响。我确信如果这样的报道不加以控制，那么将会对个人和社会均产生不利影响。

unlawful [ˌʌnˈlɔːful] *adj.* 不法的，违法的；不道德的

拓 lawful *adj.* 合法的； unlawfully *adv.* 不合法地

同 illegal *adj.* 非法的，违法的

用 unlawful activities 非法活动

unlawful interests 非法利益

例 He was arrested for the unlawful possession of fire arms. 他因非法携带武器而被捕。

legal [ˈliːgəl] *adj.* 法律的，合法的，法定的

拓 legality *n.* 合法，合法性

同 lawful *adj.* 合法的，法定的

licit *adj.* 合法的； legitimate *adj.* 合法的

反 illegal *adj.* 非法的，违法的

用 legal aid 法律援助

legal effect 法律效力

legal obligation 法律义务

legal right 合法权利，法定权利

legal services 法律服务

例 It is not legal for boys of that age to drink alcohol. 这个年龄的男孩喝酒是违法的。

misdeed [misˈdiːd] *n.* 不端行为，违法行为

同 error *n.* 错误，过失； offense *n.* 犯罪，过错

delinquency/fault *n.* 错误

例 You should not have sold the car in that unsafe condition; sooner or later your misdeeds will come home to roost. 你不该把存在安全隐患的车卖掉，这种不道德的行为迟早会得到报应。

misdemeanor [ˌmisdiˈmiːnə] *n.* 轻罪；品行不端

例 He is charged with several misdemeanors, including driving without a valid licence and creating a disturbance. 他被控告犯有几种轻罪，其中包括无照驾驶和扰乱治安。

sentence ['sentəns] *n.&vt.* 判决，宣判

用 be sentenced to death 被判处死刑

例 Compare the sentence-extension with other solutions, which is the best way for public security?
延长刑期和其他解决方式相比，哪一个方式是保障公共安全的最好办法？

trespass ['trespəs] *vi.* 侵入，犯罪，冒犯；*n.* 罪过

同 encroach *vi.* 侵占；*vt.*侵犯
infringe *vt.* 侵犯，破坏；*vi.* 侵犯
intrude *vi.* 侵扰
invade *vt.* 侵扰；*vi.* 侵犯

用 trespass upon someone's land
未经许可进入某人的地界
trespass on someone's time 占用某人的时间

例 The fishing boat was seized for its trespassing into restricted waters.
渔船因非法侵入受限制的水域而被扣押。

infringement [in'frindʒmənt] *n.* 侵犯，违反

同 offense *n.* 犯罪，过错；invasion *n.* 侵犯，入侵

用 patent infringement 专利侵权

例 Personal information gets severe infringement and abuse in the process of China's informationisation, so constituting personal information law for protecting personal information is extremely urgent.
在我国的信息化过程中，个人信息受到了严重的侵害和滥用，制定个人信息法来保护个人信息的权利迫在眉睫。

culpable ['kʌlpəbl] *adj.* 应受谴责的，有罪的

同 blamable *adj.* 应受谴责的； guilty *adj.* 有罪的
faulty *adj.* 有错误的

例 The judge found the man culpable.
法官认为那个人有罪。

embezzlement [im'bezlmənt] *n.* 侵占；挪用，盗用

拓 embezzle *vt.* 盗用，挪用

用 embezzlement of funds 盗用公款

例 Serious cases of embezzlement, bribery and bureaucracy have been brought to light recently. 最近披露了相当严重的贪污、受贿和官僚主义问题。

bring to light 揭露；发现；公开

同 uncover *vt.* 揭露；*vi.* 发现
disclose *vt.* 揭露，公开

例 An old saying goes that time will bring to light whatever is hidden.
俗话说得好，时间会让隐藏的事实水落石出。

peace-making [pi:s'meikiŋ] *n.* 调停，调解；*adj.* 调停的，调解的

例 The approach allows youth to deal constructively with interpersonal conflicts, problem-solving techniques and behaviours of peace-making skills.
这种方法可以培养年轻人处理人际关系、解决问题的能力及调解问题的技巧。

law enforcement 法律的实施

例 This mechanism acts positively in enhancing the ability and efficiency of law enforcement, but it also exists some problems.
这种机制对提高执法能力和执法效率具有积极作用，但是也存在一定的问题。

ordinance ['ɔ:dinəns] *n.* 条例，法令

同 legislation *n.* 立法，法律；law *n.* 法律

regulation *n.* 规则，管理

例 We believe that the city and community would be better served by an ordinance.
我们认为法令能保证城市及社区的安定。

abide by the law 遵守法律

同 respect the law 遵守法律

例 It is important that all citizens abide by the law.
重要的是，所有公民都应该遵纪守法。

reintegrate into 重新融入

用 reintegrate into society 重新融入社会

例 We should reintegrate our nation's economy into the world economy.
我们应当将国家经济重新融入到世界经济中去。

rehabilitation ['riː(h)əˌbili'teiʃən] *n.* 恢复，康复；再教育

用 rehabilitation center 修复中心
rehabilitation project 康复工程
rehabilitation psychology 康复心理学
rehabilitation therapy 康复治疗

例 Prevention works better and is cheaper than treatment. The fact is that prevention and early intervention hold far more promise than good rehabilitation programs for actually reducing crime.
防患于未然。事实是，对于减少犯罪，预防和早期的干预要比再教育更有意义。

aspiration [ˌæspə'reiʃən] *n.* 渴望，抱负

拓 aspire *vi.* 渴望，追求

同 ambition *n.* 野心，雄心，抱负，志向

用 aspiration to knowledge 求知欲

例 Children with low intelligence are likely to do worse

in school. This may increase the chances of offending because low educational attainment, a low attachment to school, and low educational aspirations are all risk factors for offending in themselves.
智力水平较低的孩子往往在学校表现很差。因为学习成绩差、不留恋学校、对自己教育的期望值很低，这些都是导致犯罪的危险因素，因而也就加大了犯罪的机率。

attachment [ə'tætʃmənt] *n.* 情感，爱慕，依恋，眷恋

用 attachment bond 依恋情结

例 Children with a weak attachment to their parents are more likely to offend. 不太喜欢父母的人更容易犯罪。

become involved in 使卷入，使陷入

例 A minor who has a lower intelligence and who does not receive a proper education is more prone to become involved in delinquent conduct.
一些智力水平低和没有受过良好教育的年轻人更容易卷入到犯罪行为中。

multiple ['mʌltipl] *adj.* 多重的，多样的，许多的

同 manifold *adj.* 多方面的

例 In many instances, multiple individual risk factors can be identified as contributing to a juvenile's involvement in destructive and illegal activities.
在很多情况下，有多种个人冒险因素导致青少年参与具有破坏性且违法的活动。

social norms 社会规范，社会准则

用 observe social norms 遵守社会规范
conform to social norms 遵守社会规范

例 Parents who demonstrate a lack of respect for the

law and social norms are likely to have children who think similarly.

不遵守法律和社会规范的家长，也容易培养出和他们想法类似的孩子。

engage in 从事，参加

用 be engaged in 忙于，从事于

engage in a lawsuit 打官司，进行诉讼

engage oneself in sth. 忙于某事

例 Additionally, juveniles are far more likely to engage in destructive, harmful and illegal activities when using drugs and alcohol.

此外，青少年一旦沾染上毒品或是酒精，就特别容易参与破坏性、有害性且违法的活动。

divert [dai'və:t] *vt.* 转移，使……转向；*vi.* 转移

同 distract *vt.* 转移，分心

用 divert attention from 分散注意力

例 Positive intervention, through programming, education and counseling, can divert a juvenile from a path that otherwise would result in delinquency as a child and crime as an adult.

通过一些课程、教育及咨询等积极的干预手段，可以使青少年走上正轨，避免他们犯罪或长大后走上犯罪的道路。

hidden ['hidn] *adj.* 隐藏的

同 latent *adj.* 潜在的

potential *adj.* 可能的，潜在的

covert *adj.* 隐秘的，隐蔽的

例 There may also be other hidden reasons contributing to this behaviour.

也可能有其他的隐藏的原因导致这种行为。

intervention [ˌintəˈvenʃən] *n.* 介入，干预，调停；妨碍

拓 intervene *vi.* 干涉，调停

intervenient *adj.* 干涉的，调停的

例 Without intervention, this could lead to more serious problems and deteriorating behaviours.

如果没有干预，就会导致更严重的问题及更恶劣的行为。

链接机经关键词

- 青少年走上犯罪道路(embark on the criminal road)的原因是多种多样的(manifold)。

  其一是：家庭原因，例如在单亲家庭(single parent family)，缺乏家庭的关爱及正确的引导(lack of connectedness and lack of parental care)，甚至有些家庭存在着家庭暴力(domestic violence/family violence)，家长不要给孩子贴上消极意义的标签(label) 。

  其二是：社会的原因，社会的复杂性极易令孩子误入歧途(be led astray in the complicated society)。

  其三是：科技的原因，互联网和手机为犯罪提供了新的渠道 (a new avenue for committing crimes)。

  其四是：学校的原因，学生承受同伴带来的压力及学业压力、竞争压力(peer pressure and study pressure, the heated competition) 。

  其五是：媒体原因，包括电视、电影、广告在内的媒体所展现的暴力和血腥的场面(the violent scenes on the media，pornographic or vulgar forms of media)，会对孩子的思想和行为带来影响。

10 动物题材

考点回顾

20100318	关闭动物园
20100220	动物园的功能
20080202	人类使用动物
20050917	动物试验

animal rights （复）动物权利，动物权益

用 animal rights groups 动物权益组织

animal rights laws 动物权利法

例 However, many animal rights activists are not happy with animals being forced to live in unnatural conditions. 然而，很多动物权利保护者对动物被迫生活在非自然的环境中表示不满。

animal welfare 动物福利

例 Although some regulations and principles have been welcomed as a step forwards by some animal welfare groups, they have also been criticized as both outdated by current research, and of little practical effect in improving animal welfare.

尽管有些法规受到动物福利组织的欢迎，认为在保护动物方面向前迈进了一步，但仍然遭到质疑，因为当前的一些动物试验已经过时，对于提高动物福利也没有什么实质性意义。

思路拓展

一些动物权利保护者认为，尽管从根本上来说，将动物用于食用、娱乐或科学研究没有什么错，但仍应立法保障这些动物免受不必要的痛苦。这种观点被称为“动物福利主义”，也是某些老牌动物保护组织所持的观点，这些组织中包括英国皇家预防虐畜协会。

animal abuse 虐待动物

同 abuse of animals 虐待动物

例 Animal rights advocates in other countries believe strict regulations are required to reduce animal abuse. 国外提倡动物权利者认为应制定一套严格的规范，以减少虐待动物的行为。

animal experimentation 动物试验

同 animal testing 动物试验；animal research 动物试验

例 They believe that if animal experimentation is stopped, then it will be at the expense of life and the human health. 他们认为如果禁止进行动物实验，那么将付出的代价是人类的健康和生命。

humane [hju'mein] *adj.* 仁慈的，人道的，高尚的

反 inhumane *adj.* 不人道的

例 It is believed that these regulations will ensure that animal research is carried out in as humane and as ethical manner as possible. However, these regulations are also under a lot of argumentation. 人们认为一些法规应该确保动物实验尽可能是人道的并符合道德规范。然而这些规定确实存在很大的争议。

test on 在……做试验

用 test on the animals 对动物做试验

例 Across the world, new products ranging from cancer

drugs to soaps and shampoos are tested on the animals. 世界上的新产品，从抗癌药品到肥皂及洗发水，都是先在动物身上做试验。

experiment on 对……进行试验，试用

同 experiment upon 试验； test on 试验

用 perform experiments on animals 在动物身上做试验

例 On the other side of the debate, those in favor of animal testing hold that experiments on animals are necessary to advance medical and biological knowledge.
辩论的另一方，动物实验的支持者认为动物实验对促进医学和生物的知识是很有必要的。

ethical ['eθikəl] *adj.* 伦理的，道德的

用 in ethical manner 以道德的方式

例 There are also objections on an ethical basis, contending that the benefits to humans do not justify the harm to animals. 也有从伦理道德角度上持反对意见的，认为对人类的益处不能合理地解释为什么要对动物进行伤害。

on moral grounds 基于道义，从道德上说

例 Some animal rights activists argue that we should ban animal experiments completely because subjecting animals to experimentation is unjustifiable on moral grounds. 一些动物权利保护者认为应该全面禁止动物试验，因为对动物进行实验从道义上说是不合理的。

ecological equilibrium 生态平衡

同 ecological balance 生态平衡
natural balance 自然平衡
equilibrium of ecosystem 生态平衡

例 We should treat animals with a humane attitude because

they are important in preserving nature's ecological equilibrium. 我们应该用一种人道的方式来对待动物，因为动物在维持自然平衡上起着重要的作用。

alternative methods 替代的方法

例 Computer simulation may be the alternative method of the animal testing.
电脑模拟可能会成为动物实验的替代方法。

barbaric [bɑːˈbærik] *adj.* 野蛮的

同 barbarian *adj.* 野蛮的，未开化的

例 It is unethical and barbaric to abuse animals.
虐待动物是不道德和野蛮的做法。

outlaw [ˈautlɔː] *vt.* 禁止，取缔；使不合法

例 People who feel a connection with animals are more likely to support programs to protect natural habitats and outlaw hunting.
人们如果和动物有感情，就更可能会支持那些保护天然栖息地和禁猎的计划。

brainwash [ˈbreinwɔʃ] *vt.* 对人洗脑，以宣传说服；*n.* 洗脑

拓 brainwashing *n.* 洗脑

用 brainwash into 把思想强行灌输给，强迫……相信

例 The general belief in the goodness of animal testing is basically the result of brainwashing that the general public has been subjected to for a long time. 认为动物实验能带来益处的想法是大众长期被洗脑的结果。

captivity [kæpˈtiviti] *n.* 囚禁，关押，监禁

拓 capture *vt.* 俘获，夺得

用 in captivity 圈养的，关闭

例 The different reasons behind keeping animals in captivity may be education, research, recreation and conservation.

将动物关起来的原因可能是出于教育、研究、娱乐对其进行保护。

poach [pəutʃ] *vt.&vi.* 偷猎，侵犯

拓 poacher *n.* 偷猎者； poaching *n.* 非法狩猎

用 poach for 偷猎

例 With an increase in poaching of wild species for skins, ivory and supposed medicinal purposes, zoos seem to be a safe haven for them.
为了获取野生物种的毛皮、象牙及药用目的，非法打猎日益增多，动物园就好像是他们的安全港湾。

breach [bri:tʃ] *n.* 违背，违反；*vt.* 违反

用 breach a contract 违约

例 Animals have natural rights and capturing them for any reason whatsoever is the breach of the same.
动物有自然（生存）的权利，无论以任何原因猎捕动物都是对其权利的侵犯。

plight [plait] *n.* 困境，境况

同 predicament *n.* 窘况，困境

用 the plight of… ……的困境

例 More and more people come to realize the plight of rare animals around the world, both in the wild and in captivity. 越来越多的人逐渐意识到无论是野生的还是圈养的珍稀野生动物都面临困境。

abnormal behaviour 异常行为，变态行为

例 No matter how good the facilities are provided in zoos, the animals are bound to suffer. Animals undergo tremendous stress as their natural movements are limited by the boundaries of the zoo. It shows up in their abnormal behaviour.

无论动物园内的设施多么完备，动物肯定是要承受痛苦的。动物的本能活动受到动物园的局限，而要承受巨大的痛苦和压力。通常行为表现异常。

endangered [in'deindʒəd] *adj.* 有生命危险的，濒临灭绝的

拓 endanger *vt.* 危及，使遭到危险

endangerment *n.* 危害

用 endangered animal species 濒危动物物种

endangered breed 濒危品种

endangered species 濒临绝种的动植物

endangered wildlife 濒危野生动物

例 The government passed new laws to protect the endangered animals from hunters. 政府通过了新法令，保护濒危物种免于猎杀。

写作提示

环境类话题动物物种的消失，小语种的消亡话题。

同义短语: be threatened with extinction, become extinct, be in peril, shrink, prevent… from dying out

Nearly half of the languages spoken in the world are considered endangered. One of the principal causes of this is the rise of English as a global language.

在世界上的语言中，几乎有一半被认为濒临消亡，其中最主要的原因之一是英语日渐成为一门全球性的语言。

endangered species 濒临灭绝的动植物

用 save endangered species 拯救濒临灭绝的动植物

例 Today's zoos put more emphasis on educational and conservation purpose than mere recreation. Many schools visit zoos to know more about endangered species and the ways to conserve them. Zoos are in fact trying to make people aware of their ecology.

现在的动物园与纯娱乐相比，更关注教育和保护的目的。很多学校组织活动参观动物园，就是为了让学生更多地了解濒危物种及保护物种的方法。事实上，动物园在提醒人们保护生态。

applied research 应用研究

拓 clinical research 临床研究
medical research 医学研究

例 It includes biology, behavioural studies, as well as applied research such as biomedical research, xenotransplantation, drug testing and toxicology tests and cosmetics testing.
动物试验包括生物学、行为学研究的纯科学，也包括像生物医药研究、异种器官移植、药品试验、毒物学及化妆品试验等的应用科学。

vaccine ['væksi:n] *n.* 疫苗

例 Testing on animals has helped develop vaccines for many life threatening diseases.
动物实验有助于研发对生命产生威胁的疫苗。

breeding ['bri:diŋ] *vt.&n.* 繁殖

用 breeding ground 滋生地，繁殖地

例 Animals are also used for education, breeding, and defense research.
动物也可以用在教学中、动物繁殖及防御（疾病）研究中。

model ['mɔdəl] *vt.* 模拟，塑造，模仿

例 National Academy of Sciences argue that even sophisticated computers are unable to model interactions between molecules, cells, tissues, organs, organisms, and the environment, making animal research necessary in many areas. 国家科学院认为即使使用精密的计算机也无法模拟出分子、细胞、组织、器官、有机体及环境间的相互作用，动物试验在很多领域都是有必要的。

vivisection [ˌviviˈsekʃən] *n.* 活体解剖

用 vivisectionist *n.* 活体解剖者
antivivisectionist *n.* 反对活体解剖者

例 Animal physiology could be affected by pain during vivisection, rendering results unreliable.
在动物实验过程中，动物承受着巨大的痛苦，使其生理机能受到严重的影响，致使实验结果不可信。

prohibit [prəˈhibit] *vt.* 阻止，禁止

拓 prohibition *n.* 禁止，禁令
prohibitive *adj.* 禁止的

同 prevent *vt.* 预防，阻止；*vi.* 阻止
ban *vt.* 禁止，取缔；*n.* 禁令，禁忌

用 prohibit sb. from doing sth. 禁止某人做某事

例 *The Wild Animals Protection Ordinance* prohibits the hunting of wild animals or the possession, sale or export of protected wild animals.
《野生动物保护条例》严禁狩猎野生动物，也禁止饲养、买卖或出口受保护的野生动物。

frown on/upon 反对，不赞成

同 be oppose to 反对；disapprove of 反对，不赞成

例 Although animal experimentation sounds appealing to some extent, I still strongly frown on this proposal.
尽管动物实验听起来具有一定的吸引力，但是我仍然强烈反对。

extinct [iksˈtiŋkt] *adj.* 灭绝的，绝种的

拓 extinctive *adj.* 使灭绝的，使绝种的

extinction *n.* 消失

用 go extinct 灭绝

例 It is our duty to save endangered animals of the world from being extinct.

我们有责任挽救濒危物种，免其灭绝。

on the brink of extinction 将要，濒于，将陷于（灾难，死亡或其他）

同 on the brim of extinction 濒于灭绝

例 Conservation efforts have already brought many animals back on the brink of extinction, but still, our work is far from done.

保护工作已经挽救了很多即将灭绝的物种，但我们还有很多工作需要做。

encroachment [inˈkrəutʃmənt] *n.* 侵入，侵犯

拓 encroach *vi.* 侵占，蚕食；*vt.* 侵犯

encroaching *adj.* 渐渐渗入的

例 Encroachment near the sea destroyed their breeding sites. 海边上（建起的宾馆和度假村）侵占了它们的繁殖地。

wildlife conservation 野生生物保护

例 It is good that there is more awareness about wildlife conservation these days and people have now realized that it is important to maintain the planet's biodiversity.

目前人们已经提高了野生动物保护的意识，并且认识到维护地球的生物多样性是重要的。

captive breeding 人工繁殖

例 Forestry and habitat protection, captive breeding, setting up more nature reserves and parks can save the endangered animals from being extinct.

保护林区及栖息地，人工繁殖，建立更多的自然保护区及园区，都能够保护濒危物种避免灭绝。

die out 灭绝；消失

例 It is reported that there are about 5,000 endangered animals and at least one species dies out every year.
据报道，世界大约有5000种的濒危动物，每年至少有一种动物灭绝。

mutilation [ˌmjuːtiˈleiʃən] *n.* 毁损，残缺；切断

拓 mutilate *vt.* 切断，毁坏

例 It is totally unconscionable to subject defenseless animals to mutilation and death.
使毫无抵抗能力的动物遭受残缺断肢之痛甚至是死亡，这种做法真是丧尽天良。

compassion [kəmˈpæʃən] *n.* 同情，怜悯

拓 compassionate *adj.* 富于同情心的，慈悲的；*vt.* 同情

例 Compassion for animals is intimately connected with goodness of character and it may be confidently asserted that he who is cruel to animals cannot be a good man. 对动物是否怀有悲悯之情是与人善良的性格密切相关的，也可以确切地说对待动物残忍的人，不可能是好人。

链接机经关键词

⊙ 动物实验 Animal experimentation

人类在很多科学实验(scientific experiment)和医学实验(medical research)的过程及临床研究(clinical research)中，都会先在动物身上做试验(animal experimentation/testing)，其行为是残忍和野蛮的

(cruel and barbaric)，也是不人道的(inhumane)。动物也有生存权(animal rights)，应该与人类共存(coexistence)。因此，在科学发达的今天，人类应该尽量寻求一些可替代的方式(alternative methods)来进行实验，如电脑模拟(computer model)。

动物与动物园(Animals and zoos)

很多濒危的动物(endangered animals) 面临着灭绝的境地(extinguished/extinct)，可是人们还是进行非法打猎(poaching)，破坏自然栖息地(damage natural habitat)，因而可能将动物关在动物园里是一个无奈之举，那么动物园有何利弊(merit and demerit)。

在动物园中能够提供专业的看管(professional care and treatment)。同时动物园也是进行科学研究和物种繁殖的场所(a scientific research center and a place for the breeding)；动物园也起着一定的教育功能(play an educational role)，丰富参观者的知识(enrich visitors' knowledge and widen their horizon)。此外，动物园也是人们娱乐和放松的场所(a place of entertainment)。

动物与人（Animals and human）

动物是人类的朋友(good friends of mankind)，是生态系统中不可缺少的一部分(an indispensable part in nature)；动物是人类的伙伴(companion)，同时动物有助于培养孩子们对大自然的热爱(nurture the love for nature)，培养孩子的爱心(love and care)、责任心(sense of responsibility)和独立精神(independence)，有利于驱赶人们的孤独(drive off the loneliness)，尤其可以陪伴(accompany)退休后的老年人。

Unit 3

逻辑词汇联盟

本单元主要介绍了雅思写作中的逻辑词汇。雅思作文的一大评分标准是逻辑词汇的恰当使用，即作文是不是连贯。逻辑词汇就像路标词，一段英文单词像是一颗颗珍珠，如果没有线来穿引，这些珍珠势必会大珠小珠落玉盘，作文里的逻辑词汇就好比是这根线。本单元主要从顺序展开、并列关系、举例论证、因果关系、比较与对比、条件关系、让步转折、解释说明、强调手法、细化主题、定义手法和总结用语等方面来介绍逻辑词汇。

1 顺序展开

firstly ['fə:stli] *adv.* 首先，第一（主要用于列举条目、论点时）

同 in the first place 首先
first and foremost 首要的是
to begin with 首先
to start with 首先
initially *adv.* 首先

例 Firstly, a child will learn to interact with a lot of different people and some children learn to communicate very early because of this.
首先，孩子要学习与很多不同的人打交道，有些孩子因为这一点很早就学会了沟通。

first of all 首先

例 First of all, eggs are produced by the moth and it takes ten days for each egg become silkworm larva that feeds on mulberry leaves.
首先，蛾产卵，经过十天的时间，卵孵化成蚕幼虫，这些幼虫以桑叶为食。

begin by 以……开始，首先

同 start by 以……开始，首先

用 begin by doing sth. 从做……开始

例 I would like to begin by pointing out that traditional skills and ways of life are not automatically of one country, but of a culture or community. 首先，我要指

出传统技术和生活方式不单单是属于某一国家的，而是属于某一种文化和区域的。

in addition 另外，此外

同 secondly *adv.* 其次，第二

in the second place 其次，第二

furthermore *adv.* 此外，而且

what is more 而且

additionally *adv.* 此外

例 In addition, the Internet, and modern refrigeration techniques, are being used to keep alive the traditional skills of producing salmon.

此外，互联网和现代制冷技术的运用使传统制作大马哈鱼的手艺保存下来。

furthermore [ˈfəːðəˌmɔː] *adv.* 此外，而且

同 what is more 此外，而且

in addition 另外，此外

additionally *adv.* 此外

例 Furthermore, the majority of stars do not hold their top positions long.

此外，大部分明星的职业巅峰状态不会太长。

eventually [iˈventʃuəli] *adv.* 最后，终于

同 lastly *adv.* 最后；in the final place 最后

last but not least 最后；finally *adv.* 终于，最后

to end with 最后；last of all 最后

in the final analysis 最后

例 After a period of about three weeks, the adult moths eventually emerge from these cocoons and the life cycle begins again.

经过三周左右的时间，成年的飞蛾最终脱离蚕茧，生命周而复始。

2 并列关系

as well 也，同样地

例 There are health and safety issues to be considered as well. 健康和安全问题也要考虑。

as well as 也，和……一样

例 Finally, I think it is very important to remember that children need to relax as well as work.
最后我认为要记住孩子们需要工作，也需要放松身心，这些是很重要的。

neither...nor 既不……也不……

例 In some cases an employee is working in a job that suits neither their skills nor their personality.
有些情况下，员工所从事白工作既不能发挥他的技能长处，也不能发挥他的性格长处。

or [ɔː] *conj.* 或者，还是

例 Secondly, when someone feels they are improving or developing their skills through training opportunities, then there is a sense of progress and purpose that rewards a worker. 其次，如果人们通过培训能够不断地提升自己的技能，那么他们就能够感到自己在进步，这是对自己的一种回馈。

either...or... 二者择一的，要么……要么……

例 However, he stressed that a slowdown in either the U. S. or China would affect both economies.
不过他强调，无论是美国还是中国的增长减速都

会对双方经济产生影响。

not only...but also... 不仅……而且……

例 The trend is not only restricted to rich students who have the money to travel, but is also evident among poorer students who choose to work and become economically independent for a period of time.
这一趋势不仅表现在有钱出去旅游的学生身上，而且一些家境不是很富裕的学生也选择工作以获得经济上的独立。

both...and... 两个都，既……又……

例 Parental love is expected to offer both financial support and emotional fulfillment. 父母的爱体现在既要给予孩子经济支持，又要从情感上给予关怀。

whether...or 无论是……还是……，或者……或者……

例 It is difficult to say who has the right to judge whether children working is wrong or valuable.
很难说谁有权力来评判孩子们工作是错误的还是有价值的。

for one thing...for another... 一方面……另外一方面……

用 Confronted with..., we should take a series of effective measures to... For one thing...For another...
面临……我们应该采取一系列行之有效的方法来……，一方面……另一方面……

例 For one thing, it is everyone's duty to protect the environment. For another, the teachers and parents should be the role-models for the children in this respect.
一方面，每个人都有责任来保护环境；另一方面，老师和家长也应该在这方面为孩子做个榜样。

3. 举例论证

including [in'klu:diŋ] *prep.* 包含，包括

例 Obviously, education systems are based on the belief that all children can be taught to acquire different skills, including those associated with sport, art or music.
很明显，教育体制的基本理念是让孩子学会包括体育、艺术或音乐在内的各种不同技能。

such as 例如，比如，像……那样的

例 The application of cloning can afford many possible ways and methods for mankind to solve the confronted problems such as population, resources, energy, food, environment and health. 克隆技术的应用为解决人类面临的人口、资源、能源、粮食，环境与健康等问题提供了多种可能的途径和方法。

specifically [spə'sifikli] *adv.* 特别地，具体来说

同 to be specific 具体来说

例 Specifically, France spends more on CDs and photographic film but less on tennis racquets than Italy does. 具体来说，法国在唱片和胶卷上的花销比意大利多，但在网球拍上的花费比意大利少。

to name but a few 仅举数例

例 Many of the vegetables found in today's markets come from other countries—strawberries from Mexico, asparagus from Peru and carrots from Canada, to name but a few. 现在市场上的很多蔬菜都是从国外运

过来的，举几个例子，像来自墨西哥的草莓，来自秘鲁的芦笋和来自加拿大的胡萝卜。

a case in point 恰当的例子

例 Some children are selfish and the unwillingness to help their friend is a case in point. 有些孩子很自私，不愿意帮助朋友就是一个明显的例子。

as an illustration 例如，举例说明

同 to illustrate 举例说明

例 As an illustration, many countries are getting globalized at a staggering rate. 例如，很多国家正以一种惊人的速度迈向全球化。

illustrate ['iləstreit] *vt.* 阐明，举例说明；*vi.* 举例

用 it can be illustrated that… 通过……来证明

例 Technology can reshape people's life and it can be illustrated that mobile phones have changed the ways of communication among people.
科技能够重新塑造人们的生活，手机改变了人们之间的沟通方式，就足以证明这一点。

illustrious [i'lʌstriəs] *adj.* 著名的，杰出的

用 the most illustrious evidence is… 最明显的例证是……

例 Many young people are overly-dependent on the computer games and the most illustrious evidence is that they live in a virtual life.
很多年轻人过度依赖电脑游戏，最明显的例证是他们过着虚拟的生活。

take…as an example 以……为例

例 Take big cities as an example, roads are still packed with cars, and traffic congestion still exists. 就拿大城市来说，路上依然挤满了汽车，交通堵塞依然存在。

convincing example 令人信服的例子

用 sth. serves as a convincing example
……是令人信服的例子

例 Lack of the awareness of environmental protection leads directly to severe destruction of the eco-system, and the worsening air pollution serves as a convincing example. 缺乏环境保护的意识会直接导致生态系统的严重破坏，日益严重的空气污染就是一个铁证。

cite sth. as a convincing example of…
……是令人信服的例证

同 cite…as an excellent example of ……是很好的例证

例 Besides the motorized flight, we can cite the wide spread use of mobile phones as a convincing example of the advancement of technology in 21st century. 除了飞机之外，我们认为手机的广泛使用是21世纪科技发展的最好证明。

4. 因果关系

accordingly [ə'kɔːdiŋli] *adv.* 因此，于是

同 consequently *adv.* 所以，因此

例 Nowadays, people face fierce competition and suffer from great pressure. Accordingly, they have to devote more time and energy to their careers. 现在，人们面临着激烈的竞争并承受着极大的压力，因而，他们必须要将更多的时间和精力投入到工作中。

be attributed to 归因于……

用 One of the most contributing factors of… could be

attributed to… 一个重要的原因可以被归结为……

例 The mounting death toll from motor vehicle accidents can mainly be attributed to the glut of automobiles appearing on city roads in recent years. 车祸死亡率的上升主要归因于近年来城市道路的汽车数量骤增。

be engendered by 由……产生

例 Obviously, students' poor academic performance may be engendered by their spending too much time in employment. 很明显，学生花费过多的时间在工作上，会影响他们的学习成绩。

be the chief culprit ……是罪魁祸首

同 be the chief reason 主要原因

例 Lack of communication is the chief culprit of the alienation among families.
缺乏沟通是导致家庭成员间疏远的罪魁祸首。

be responsible for 是造成……的原因

例 Poor student behavior seems to be an increasingly widespread problem and I think that modern lifestyles are probably responsible for this. 学生行为不端的现象日益增多，我认为原因可能在于现代生活方式。

consequence ['kɔnsikwəns] *n.* 结果，后果

用 as a consequence 因此
the consequence of … ……的后果

例 But I think the solution lies with the families, who need to be more aware of the future consequences of spoiling their children. 但我认为解决方法在于家庭，家长要意识到溺爱儿童会造成的后果。

in consequence of 因为……的缘故，由于

例 Most buyers have withdrawn from the market in

consequence of unstable prices. 由于价格不稳定，大多数买主已退出市场。

have roots in 根源于，原因

例 Many of our feelings of happiness or unhappiness have their roots in how we compare ourselves with others. 许多的满足和不满足感源自于我们选择了怎样的比较对象。

contributing factor 影响因素

用 a major contributing factor to…
……的一个主要影响因素
cite…as a contributing factor
把……列为影响因素
list… as a contributing factor
把……列为影响因素

例 Nowadays, doctors are increasingly citing stress as a major contributing factor to most illnesses.
当今，医生说压力是导致大多数疾病的一个主要因素。

give rise to 使发生，引起

同 lead to 导致

例 Such conduct might give rise to misunderstanding during the travelling abroad.
在国外旅行中，这种行为可能会产生误解。

direct cause 直接原因

拓 …is the main cause of… ……是主要原因
…is the primary cause of… ……是主要原因
…is the root cause of… ……是根本原因
The root cause is… 根本原因是……
…is the principal cause of… 主要原因是……

例 It is certainly true that the position of women in society has undergone a dramatic change in the past twenty years but I do not feel that this is a direct cause of the indisputable increase in juvenile-related problems during this period. 女性的社会地位在过去的二十年间确实发生了巨大的变化，但我不认为这是这一期间青少年问题上升的直接原因。

as a result of 由于

例 As a result of constant media attention, sports professionals in our country have become stars and celebrities, and those at the top are paid huge salaries. 由于媒体的不断关注，我们国家的职业运动员成了明星和名人，那些最优秀的运动员还获得高额的收入。

result in 导致，结果是

同 lead to 导致，带来； bring about 带来
contribute to 有助于，促成

例 I do not believe that the increase in the number of working mothers has resulted in children being brought up less well than previously. 我不认为职业型母亲的增加会使得孩子的成长环境比以前差。

result from 起因于，由……造成

例 Her blindness of both eyes resulted from a traffic accident. 一次交通事故使她双目失明。

stem from 起源于

同 originate from 引起，起源于

例 The poor health mainly stems from several factors, including inappropriate diets, poor healthcare practices and the poor interpersonal relationship.

不健康的状态主要由几个因素引起，这些因素包括不适当的饮食、不好的保健习惯以及不良的人际关系。

a source of 来源

例 We also forget that it is a source of pollution and difficult to dispose of.
我们也忘记了它是一种污染源，而且很难分解。

That is why... 那就是为什么……

例 That is why, in recent years, there has been a growing body of opinion in favour of putting more resources into health education and preventive measures.
那就是为什么近些年来越来越多的人赞成将更多的资源投入到健康教育和预防措施上来。

There are some reasons why... 有一些原因……

例 In conclusion, I think there may be some reasons why entertainment stars earn high salaries but overall I agree that they are overpaid.
总之，我认为可能有一些原因造成了娱乐明星的高薪现象，但总体而言我认为他们收入过高。

because of 因为，由于

例 Feelings about one's job must reflect how an individual feels about his or her life as a whole, and because of this, job satisfaction is indeed very important for the wellbeing of that person.
对工作的感受也能从整体上反映出个人对生活的感受，因此，对工作的满意度对一个人的幸福来说确实至关重要。

partly because 部分原因在于……

用 This is partly because... 部分原因在于……

...partly because... ……部分原因在于……

例 This is partly because sitting in front of a screen for too long can be damaging to both the eyes and the physical posture of young children, regardless of what they are using the computer for. 其中部分原因在于坐在电脑前太长时间，无论使用电脑做什么，都会对青少年的视力和身姿造成损害。

largely because 主要原因在于……

例 Many people leave their job largely because they are eager to seek a bright future.
很多人离职的主要原因是渴望寻求更好的未来。

This is because... 这是因为……

例 This is because it is the rich and powerful people in our society who are able to impose changes that are in their own interests. 这是因为只有社会上有钱且有权势的人才能做出符合他们利益的改变。

therefore ['ðeəfɔː] *adv.* 因此，所以

例 I think, therefore, that the governments need to raise the awareness in the general public.
因此我认为政府应该提升大众的意识。

5. 比较与对比

just like 就像，正如

例 Just like movie stars, they live extravagant lifestyles with huge houses and cars.

如同电影明星一样，他们过着奢华的生活，住着豪宅，开着名车。

likewise ['laikwaiz] *adv.* 同样地，也

例 Likewise, once they get married, the majority of women continue working since the financial pressures of setting up a house and establishing a reasonable standard of living often require two incomes.
同样地，一旦结婚，来自安家和实现适当生活水平的经济压力使得新婚家庭需要两份薪水，因此大多数的女性结婚后还是会继续工作。

alike [ə'laik] *adv.* 相像地，相似地，以同样程度

例 In fact, outdoor activities and instructive games, which enrich the children's lives, are welcomed by younger and older kids alike. 事实上，户外活动和有教育意义的游戏，能够丰富孩子们的生活，因此这些活动受到各个年龄段孩子的欢迎。

similar ['similə] *adj.* 相似的

用 be similar to 和……相似

例 Meanwhile, France and Italy generally maintain middle positions, averaging approximately similar spending overall.
同时，法国和意大利大体上保持中间水平，它们的总体花费水平很相似。

in the same manner 同样地，以同样的方式

同 in the same way 同样地，以同样的方式

例 Actually, parents are the role-models in life, for the children will behave in the same manner.
事实上，家长在生活中是孩子们的榜样，因为孩子们会以同样的方式做事。

the same as 与……一样

例 Geniuses are the luckiest of mortals because what they must do is the same as what they most want to do.
天才是人类中最幸运的人，因为他们必须要做的事与他们最想做的事相同。

compare to 比较，对比

例 In terms of the number of years of schooling received, we see that the length of time people spend at school in industrialized countries was much greater than 8.5 years in 1980, compared to 2.5 years in developing countries. 就受教育的时间而言，可以看出与发展中国家的2.5年相比，工业化发达的国家花在教育上的时间比1980年超出8.5年之多。

compare with 与……相比较

例 Compared with adults, the kids lack of experiences.
与成年人相比，孩子缺乏阅历。

in comparison 相比之下，与……比较

用 in comparison to 与……比较
in comparison with 与……比较

例 In comparison, online shopping is still a new thing in China. 相比之下，在我国网上购物还是一个新生的事物。

by contrast 相比之下，与之相比

同 in contrast 相比之下

例 By contrast, those who have spent some time earning a living or traveling to other places, have a broader view of life and better personal resources to draw on.
相比之下，花一些时间去赚钱或者到其他地方旅游的人，会有更广的见识和更好的人脉。

previously ['priːviəsli] *adv.* 以前

例 Indeed it could be argued that by giving mothers the opportunity to work and earn extra money children can be better provided for than previously.
妈妈们有机会工作赚些额外的钱，确实会给孩子提供比以前更好的生活。

on the other hand 另一方面

例 Bad news on the other hand is so common that in order to cope with it, we often simply ignore it.
从另一方面来看负面新闻如此平常，以至于我们对待负面消息的方式就是忽略它们。

conversely ['kɔnvəːsli] *adv.* 相反地

例 Conversely, a sensible approach would be to take into account students' academic performances and personality. 相反地，合理的办法是充分考虑学生的学习成绩和个性。

while [hwail] *conj.* 虽然，然而

同 whereas *conj.* 然而； whilst *conj.* 然而

例 Italy's spending on personal stereos is only marginally greater than that of France, while spending on toys is equal between the two. 意大利在个人音响上面的花销刚刚超出法国，而二者在玩具上面的花销持平。

6. 条件关系

If..., then... 如果……那么……

例 If the factors identified above are implemented, then

any job can be improved and more workers can feel greater degrees of job satisfaction.
如果上文所分析的提高工作满意的因素得以实施，那么不管什么样的工作，都会有更多的员工获得更大程度的满足感。

providing [prə'vaidiŋ] *conj.* 假如，以……为条件

例 Providing all the computers are working correctly, nothing can go wrong.
如果所有的计算机都运转正常，就不会出错。

providing that 只要

同 provided that 只要

例 All can study by relying on internet resources, regardless of their race, nationality and gender, providing that they could have access to the Internet.
所有人都可以借助互联网资源来学习，不论其种族、国籍、性别，只要他们能接入互联网。

as long as 如果，只要，在……情形下

例 Work is likely to become more demanding, and competition fiercer, but as long as graduates are fully prepared, the prospect looks promising for them.
工作的要求越来越高，竞争日益激烈，但是只要毕业生做好充分的准备，就会有美好的前景。

supposing [sə'pəuziŋ] *conj.* 假使，假如

例 Supposing the diverse species are extinct, what should we do in order to maintain the balance of the ecosystem? 如果不同的物种都灭绝了，我们该如何维护生态系统的平衡?

on condition that 如果

例 Everyone will succeed in one profession or another

on condition that sustained effort is made.
只要付出不懈的努力，每个人都会在某个领域获得成功。

7 » 让步转折

however [hau'evə] *conj.* 然而，可是

例 However, sports salaries are not determined by considering the contribution to society a person makes. 然而，运动员的收入不是由他们对社会的贡献所决定。

写作提示

however的位置很灵活，可放在句前或句中。

but [bʌt] *conj.* 但是，然而；*adv.* 仅仅，只；*prep.* 除……以外

例 They will bring a lot of benefits but they will also increase the potential risk.
他们会带来很多的益处，但也会增加潜在的风险。

instead of 代替，而不是

用 instead of sth.(doing sth.) 而不是……

例 People should be encouraged to take cloth bags to the grocery store instead of using paper or plastic bags.
应该鼓励人们去杂货店购物时带上布袋，而不是使用纸袋或是塑料袋。

otherwise ['ʌðəwaiz] *adv.* 要不然，否则

用 and otherwise 等等，及其他

or otherwise 或相反，或其反面

otherwise than 不像，除……外，与……不同

cannot be otherwise than 只能

例 Otherwise, we will pay a high price for the environmental pollution if the present situation still goes like this.
否则，如果目前的情况还这样继续下去，那么我们将会为环境污染付出更高的代价。

rather ['rɑːðə] *adv.* 相反

例 Rather, he should share those daily duties, spend as much time as his job allows with his children, play with them, read to them, help directly with their education, participate very fully in their lives and encourage them to share his.
相反，他应该分担日常事务，在工作允许的情况下尽可能经常陪孩子，与孩子玩耍，给他们读故事，在学习上辅导他们，充分融入到他们的生活之中，鼓励他们分享自己的故事。

other than 除了，不同于

例 It is important to remember that children need to develop skills other than intellectual ones, and the best way to do this is through activities such as sports, games and playing with other kids.
要记住孩子们除了要拓展知识，还需要培养各种技能，而通过体育、游戏及与其他孩子玩耍，这样的活动是培养孩子技能的最好方法。

even when 即使当……

例 Even when people believe they are resisting change themselves, they cannot stop the world around them from changing. 即使当人们自己阻止改变时，他们也无法阻止世界的改变。

even though 虽然，即使

同 even if 虽然，即使

例 However, even though it is unlikely that all workers do feel happy in their work, I think it is not unrealistic to promote more job satisfaction in any job.
然而，虽然想让所有的员工对工作满意是不太可能的，但是我认为在任何工作中提升工作满意度不是不可实现的。

regardless of 不顾，不管

例 They are allowed to have whatever they want regardless of price. 只要他们想得到的东西，不管价格如何，他们都能得到。

in spite of 尽管，不管，不顾

例 In spite of this, the obvious benefits of computer skills for young children cannot be denied.
尽管如此，年轻人掌握计算机的技能具有不可否认的优势。

nevertheless [ˌnevəðə'les] *adv.* 然而，不过

例 Nevertheless, in better economic circumstances, few parents would choose to send their children out to do full-time paid work.
然而经济条件好的家庭，很少有父母会让孩子做全职的工作。

nonetheless [ˌnʌnðə'les] *adv.* 然而，不过

同 nevertheless *adv.* 然而，不过

例 Nonetheless, we cannot advocate the experiment on the animals for it violates the animal rights.
但是，我们不能提倡动物试验，因为这侵犯了动物的权利。

yet [jet] *adv.* 还，但是，已经；*conj.* 但是，然而

例 Teachers, nurses, laboratory researchers, etc. are never listed among the best-paid professionals, yet they are more important to our well-being and our future than the stars who earn their fortunes so quickly. 教师、护士和实验室研究人员等却从来没有被列入高薪行业之中，然而与那些赚钱如此之快的明星相比，他们对于我们的幸福和未来来说更加重要。

no matter how 不管怎样

例 No matter how experienced a speaker you are, and how well you have prepared your speech, such a noisy reception as that is apt to be very off-putting. 无论你是多么富有经验的演说家，无论你作了多么充分的准备，在这样嘈杂的招待会上你很难发表演讲。

despite [dis'pait] *prep.* 尽管，不管

用 despite the fact that 尽管……的事实

例 Despite its defects, city life still attracts more and more people to move into the city. 虽然都市生活也有弊端，但仍然吸引愈来愈多的人去城里住。

(in) despite of 尽管，不管

例 We shall be victorious in despite of difficulties. 不管有什么困难，我们一定会胜利。

whilst [wailst] *conj.* 虽然，尽管

例 I believe that child-rearing should be the responsibility of both parents and that, whilst the roles within that partnership may be different, they are nevertheless equal in importance. 我认为抚养孩子是家长双方的责任，尽管角色可能不同，然而父母双方同等重要。

8. 解释说明

to put it differently 换句话说

同 put it another way 换句话说

例 To put it differently, to eradicate poverty should be a global priority.

换句话说，全球最应注意的问题就是消除贫困。

as a matter of fact 事实上

例 As a matter of fact, the development of international tourism is in line with globalization.

事实上，跨国旅游的发展符合全球一体化的趋势。

frankly speaking 坦白来说

例 Frankly speaking, the environmental damage is the consequence of our misconception that material wealth is tantamount to a better life.

坦白地说，环境的破坏是因为我们误以为拥有丰富的物质就会拥有美好的生活。

namely ['neimli] *adv.* 也就是，即是

例 The bar chart illustrates five countries which were visited most frequently by UK residents in 1999, namely, France, Spain, USA, Greece and Turkey.

该柱状图描述了1999年法国、西班牙、美国、希腊和土耳其是英国人旅游最经常去的五个国家。

This is partly explained by the fact that...

事实多少说明了这一点

例 This is partly explained by the fact that it is dangerous

to put too much pressure on children.
事实多少说明了给孩子太多的压力是很危险的。

What is meant by this... 通过这一点说明的是

例 What is meant by this is that better academic performance contributes a great deal to children's future careers.
通过这一点想说明的是学习成绩对孩子的将来发展有很大的帮助。

This is the case... 就是这样

例 This was certainly the case in the past in many industrialized countries, and it is very difficult to judge that it is wrong for children today to contribute to the family income in this way.
过去很多工业化的国家就是这样的情况，因而很难说孩子通过这种方式来增加家庭收入是错误的。

9. 强调手法

especially [is'peʃəli] *adv.* 特别，尤其，格外

用 especially when 尤其当……的时候

例 It especially excited their inquisitiveness.
这尤其引起了他们的好奇心。

particularly [pə'tikjuləli] *adv.* 特别地，独特地

例 So far so good, but the difficulties start when we try to define what the proportion of the budget should

be, particularly if the funds will be diverted from the treatment.
到目前还好，但是当我们想明确预算是多少比例的时候，麻烦就出现了，尤其当资金从治疗费用里转走时。

in particular 尤其，特别

例 There is a growing tendency for people, young people in particular, to travel to other countries to have access to foreign culture. 越来越多的人，尤其是年轻人，到国外旅游，目的是想接触异国文化。

certainly ['sə:tnli] *adv.* 无疑地，肯定地，不可否认地

例 It is certainly very understandable that some governments should start looking at ways of limiting their populations to a sustainable figure.
可以理解的是，政府应该寻求一些解决办法将人口控制在可承受的范围内。

the very 正是

例 However, it is also true that it is only those who reach the very top of their profession who can get these huge salaries. 然而，只有那些达到事业顶峰的人才能得到如此丰厚的薪金，这也是事实。

in fact 事实上，实际上

例 While some people think this may be damaging to a child's development, or to a child's relationship with his or her parents, in fact there are many advantages to having school experience at a young age.
一些人认为这会影响孩子的发展，或者会破坏他们与父母之间的亲情。实际上，提早上学还是有很多益处的。

in effect 实际上，实质上，事实上

例 They are, in effect, rare talents.
他们确实是难得的人才。

It is…that (who)… 强调句型

例 It is the interaction of the two that shapes a person's personality and dictates how the personality develops.
正是两者的相互作用才形成人的个性，并决定着个性如何发展。

stress [stres] *vt.* 强调

用 It must be stressed out that…
应该着重指出的是……

例 It must be stressed out that the animals maintain the subtle balance of the ecological system to a large extent. 必须着重指出的一点是在很大程度上，动物能维护生态的平衡。

写作提示

表示"应该着重指出"的相关表达：
It must be pointed out that…
应该着重指出的一点是……
What is worth mentioning that… 值得一提的是……
It is worth mentioning that… 值得一提的是……

undoubtedly [ʌn'dautidli] *adv.* 确实地，毋庸置疑地

同 without doubt 毫无疑问地

例 Undoubtedly, team spirit is the vital element for a good operation of an organization. 毫无疑问，团队精神是一个团队良好运作的重要因素。

There is no denying that… 毫无疑问

同 There is no doubt that… 毫无疑问

It is undoubted that… 毫无疑问

It is undeniable that… 毫无疑问

例 There is no denying that the increasing number of the private cars is a contributing factor to the worsening air pollution.

毫无疑问的是私家车的增多是导致空气污染日益恶化的一个影响因素。

emphasise ['emfəsaiz] *vt.* 强调

拓 emphasis *n.* 强调

用 emphasise on… 强调

例 I would like to emphasise that I remain very keen to work with you, and that I will be gaining further useful experience during this time.

我想强调的一点是我非常愿意和您一起共事，在此期间我会积累更有用的经验。

10. 细化主题

as with 就……来说

例 But, as with all questions of nature versus nurture, they are not mutually exclusive.

但是就先天资质和后天培养来说，二者并不是相互矛盾的。

as to 至于，关于，就……而论

同 as for 关于，至于

例 The teacher must exercise his own discretion, as to the methods of teaching.

至于采用哪种教学方法，教师应该自行决定。

as far as...is concerned 就……而言

例 As far as the punishment of the children is concerned, the purpose is to point out the mistakes and prevent further recurrence. 就体罚孩子而言，其目的是指出错误，防止再犯。

in terms of 在……方面，就……来说，关于……

例 Perhaps parenting classes are needed to help them to do this, and high quality nursery schools could be established that would support families more in terms of raising next generation.

也许需要设立家长学校来帮助家长了解如何培养儿童，也应该建立高品质的托儿所来帮助家庭抚养小孩。

in...terms 就……而言

例 How do we accurately measure which health education campaigns are effective in both medical and financial terms?

就医疗和经济而言，我们该如何衡量哪些健康教育宣传是有效的?

in this respect 在这方面

同 in this light 从这个角度说

in this sense 在某种意义上

in this aspect 在这方面

例 Firstly, a person needs to feel that they are doing valuable work, so positive feedback from superiors is very important in this respect.

首先，个人应感到他们所从事的是有价值的工作，因而从上司那里得到积极的反馈是很重要的。

lie in 在于

同 lie with 取决于，在于

例 While some people link happiness to wealth and material success, others think it lies in emotions and loving personal relationships.
然而有些人将幸福与财富和物质上的成功联系起来，另一些人认为幸福在于情感及良好的人际关系。

when it comes to sth. 当提到……，就……而论

例 When it comes to educating the children, there are many numerous ways instead of punishment. 当谈到教育孩子的问题时，除了惩罚，还有很多方法。

regarding [ri'gɑːdiŋ] *prep.* 关于，至于

同 respecting *prep.* 关于，就……而言
considering *prep.* 考虑到，就……而论

例 We are preparing to hold a meeting to discuss problems regarding the quality of education.
关于教学质量问题，我们准备开会讨论。

11. 定义手法

mean [miːn] *vt.* 意味

用 This means that… 这就意味着……

例 Hard economic realities mean that many people have little choice in the kind of job they can get.
经济不景气对很多人来说也就意味着他们对工作没有什么选择余地。

by that I mean 我的意思是……

例 By that I mean an ability to have a clear sense of what is important in our lives and what is not.
我的意思是要有能力分清生活中什么是重要的及什么是不重要的。

it indicates that... 这说明了……

例 Personally, I think that the amount of money such sports stars make is more justified than the huge earnings of movie stars, but at the same time, it indicates that our society places more value on sport than on more essential professions and achievements.
我个人认为和影星的巨额收入相比，这些体育明星的薪酬更合理，但与此同时，这一现象表明与其他更重要的职业相比，我们社会更重视体育。

identify...as 使等同于，把……看做一致

例 They identify population control as a means to raising living standards.
他们把控制人口看作是提高生活水平的方法。

definition [ˌdefiˈniʃən] *n.* 定义

例 Because people interpret happiness for themselves in so many different ways, it is difficult to give any definition that is true for everyone.
因为人们对幸福的理解千差万别，很难给出适合于每个人的关于幸福的定义。

describe...as... 把……称为，把……说成

例 There are few people who may be described as geniuses. 很少有能称得上天才的人。

be equivalent to 相当于，等于

例 Changing her job like that is equivalent to giving her

the sack. 那样调换她的工作等于是解雇她。

be characterized by 具有……的特性，以……为特征

同 be featured by… 以……为特征

例 The present world economic relations can be characterized by the widening economic gap between the developed and the underdeveloped.
当前国际经济关系中的一个重要特点是发达与不发达国家之间经济差距仍在扩大。

be characteristic of 其特点是……

例 This restaurant seems to be characteristic of vegetarian dishes.
这家餐厅似乎是以素菜为其特色。

12 总结用语

as a whole 总的来说

例 The government should fund this kind of programme, because this is no longer a problem of individual families, but for society as a whole.
政府应该资助这种方案，因为这不仅是每个家庭的问题，也是整个社会的问题。

on the whole 一般说来，总而言之，大体上

例 On the whole, the elimination of air pollution needs the joint efforts from the government, the public and the environmentalists.
总体上来说，消除空气污染需要政府、大众及环保工作者的共同努力。

overall ['əuvərɔ:l] *adv.* 总体上，大体上，总的来说

例 Overall we can see that not only are there very large differences between the two economies but these gaps are widening.
总之，我们可以看出两种经济之间不仅存在着巨大的差距，而且差距不断扩大。

on balance 总而言之，总的说来

例 On balance, the strengths of the plan outweigh its weaknesses.
总的来说，这个计划的优点多过缺点。

generally speaking 一般说来

例 Generally speaking, youngsters tend to be more consumeristic than the elderly.
一般说来，年轻人比老年人更倾向于多消费。

in general 总之，通常；一般而言

例 In general, many students prefer to follow directions rather than make their own decisions.
总的来说，很多学生都更喜欢听从别人的指导，而不是自己做决策。

in conclusion 总之，综上所述

同 to conclude 总之

例 In conclusion, I agree that any child can be taught particular skills, but to be really good in areas such as music, art or sport, then some natural talent is required.
总之，我认为任何一个孩子都能习得某些技能，然而要在像音乐、艺术和体育方面出类拔萃，那么天赋是不可或缺的。

in brief 总之，简言之

同 in short 总之，简言之

例 In brief, detailed crime coverage in the media undermines our lives in several ways.
简言之，媒体上对于犯罪细节的报道会从几个方面破坏我们的生活。

in a nutshell 简而言之

同 in brief 简言之； to put it briefly 简而言之

例 In a nutshell, great efforts should be made to enhance the public' awareness of the environmental conservation.
简而言之，应该着力提升公众的环保意识。

to sum up 总之，概括地说

例 To sum up, we should be very careful with regard to the content of the information on the media and take measures to keep viewers from possible harmful influences of media.
总之，我们针对媒体信息内容，应该谨慎对待，并采取措施避免观众受到媒体上不良信息的影响。

by and large 大体上，总的来说

同 at large 整体上，一般地

例 The root cause for various problems faced by mankind today, by and large, lies in development.
今天人类面临的种种问题，追根溯源，大都离不开发展。

all things considered 从各方面考虑起来，总的看来

例 All things considered, the economic development should not be at the cost of environmental degradation.
总的看来，经济的发展不应该以牺牲环境为代价。